I0188237

ULTIMATE FREEDOM JOURNALING PROMPTS

The Guide for Writing Your
Dreams Into Reality

Dr. Stem
Helping Other People Excel

DR. STEM SITHEMBILE MAHLATINI

ULTIMATE FREEDOM JOURNALING PROMPTS

The Guide for Writing Your Dreams Into Reality

Copyright © 2021 Dr. Stem Sithembile Mahlatini.
All rights reserved.

ISBN: 978-0-9905718-0-3
ISBN: 0-9905718-0-7

All rights reserved. No part of this publication may be reproduced, stored in a retrieval system, or transmitted in any way by any means – electronic, mechanical, photocopy, recording, or otherwise – without the prior permissions of the copyright holder, except by reviewer who may quote brief passages in a review to be printed in magazine newspaper or by radio / TV announcement, as provided by USA copyright law. The author and the publisher will not be held responsible for any errors within the manuscript. All characters appearing in this work are fictitious. Any resemblance to real persons, living or dead is purely coincidental.

Written by: Dr. Stem Sithembile Mahlatini
Drstem14@gmail.com | www.drstemspeaks.com
https://www.drstemmie.com/
Facebook: DrStem Mahlatini Twitter: DrStemahlatini
LinkedIn: Drstem Mahlatini Skype: Dr.Mahlatini

Foreword by: Dr.Stem Sithembile Mahlatini
Cover Design by: Masimba Mukundinashe.

Category: Category: Journal, Journaling, Notebooks & Writing Pads, Diary, Motivational, Inspirational, Educational and Empowerment

Printed in the USA

Foreword

I first wrote in a journal when I was 15 after a heartbreak and to be honest, I didn't write again for years until I was in graduate school and life again was getting overwhelming.

We were taught about "journaling" our thoughts, feelings and emotions to release stress during graduate school. I was hooked. I then made it a part of my coaching and counseling practice where I assigned a few journal questions related to where the client was stuck, and it worked like a charm.

My journals are my best friend, constant companions who would never ever let me down. I have many of them including ones I can lock with a key. They are like my secret sanctuary where I can express and keep my innermost thoughts.

My journals have become my personal sandbox where I can be creative and play with words and ideas. **It's in the pages of my journal that I continue to evolve and discover my passion for writing and living my best life. In addition, my journals have also become my portable therapist.**

They are on call 24/7. This is where I can speak the unspeakable and put words to my painful moments and joyful ones.

Journaling allows me to work through my pain and grief, like nothing else can. I hope and pray with these journaling prompts you too can find your own relief, peace, success and everlasting peace and joy in your life.

Through Journaling I can say I have been able to bring back my vivid visions, dreams, and aspirations. The running dialogue in my head is positive and realistic again. I am so excited because, "This Big Dreamer is Dreaming Big and Acting Boldly Again'. And, I must say, it Feels Really Good!

I know that there is way more that life has for me and I must keep writing, and believing in the process of life.

Will you follow along?

I went to town and covered questions to help you write about every aspect of your life. After this I can't wait for your own book, titled "This is my Life, My Story by ....."

which will be a sign of your rebirth. It will be the result of your new baldness and boldness.

To my parents, Benjamin and Idah Mahlatini, my heroes and greatest supporters thank you for giving me life.

My siblings, nieces and nephews, I can only be the best me I can be so that you can be the best you. Be your best and everything will work out. To all my supporters, followers, and prayer warriors, may God open up doors for you like never before, Be Encouraged and Encouraging.

After reading this book and writing your answers, I look forward to hearing your story and how you were able to boldly make decisions that have changed your life for the better by living fearlessly and free.

Contact me via E-mail if you would like me to interview you on my radio show **"The DrStem Show & Podcast"** aired on YouTube & Facebook.

You've Only got three choices in life: Give Up, Give in or Give it all you've got.

*The **Ultimate Freedom Journaling** is the answer to the Famous Question: **So what do I write about?***

Contents

1. **Introduction:** The Benefits of Journaling 8

2. **Journaling Prompts For:** Self Discovery 22

3. **Journaling Prompts For:** Letting Go 36

4. **Journaling Prompts For:** Self-Care 46

5. **Journaling Prompts For:** Burnout 64

6. **Journaling Prompts For:** Employees 72

7. **Journaling Prompts For:** Business Owners 78

8. **Journaling Prompts For:** Pursuing Success 86

9. **Journaling Prompts For:** Attracting Love 92

10. **Journaling Prompts For:** Positive Thinking 98

11. **Journaling Prompts For:** Relationships & Marriage..... 110

12. **Journaling Prompts For:** Managing Anger 116

13. **Journaling Prompts For:** Depression 122

14. **Journaling Prompts For:** Anxiety 130

15. **Journaling Prompts For:** Stress & Anxiety 138

16. **Journaling Prompts For:** Financial Prosperity..............146

17. **Journaling Prompts For:** The Grateful Heart.................154

18. Journaling Prompts For: New Beginnings 158

19. Journaling Prompts For: Building Resiliency................. 162

20. Journaling Prompts For: Healing From Hurt 166

21. Journaling Prompts For: Pursuing A Joyful Life 170

22. Journaling Prompts For: Breaking Pride 174

23. Journaling Prompts For: Being Still 178

24. Journaling Prompts For: Goal Setting 182

25. Journaling Prompts For: Getting In Touch With Your
Spiritual Side 186

26. Self-Interview Questions: Getting To Know Yourself
Better.. 190

Appendix: 192

Terms & Conditions
LEGAL NOTICE

The Publisher has strived to be as accurate and complete as possible in the creation of this report, notwithstanding the fact that he does not warrant or represent at any time that the contents within are accurate due to the rapidly changing nature of the Internet.

While all attempts have been made to verify information provided in this publication, the Publisher assumes no responsibility for errors, omissions, or contrary interpretation of the subject matter herein. Any perceived slights of specific persons, peoples, or organizations are unintentional.

In practical advice books, like anything else in life, there are no guarantees of income made. Readers are cautioned to reply on their own judgment about their individual circumstances to act accordingly.

This book is not intended for use as a source of mental health treatment, medical, legal, business, accounting or financial advice. All readers are advised to seek services of competent professionals in mental, medical, legal, business, accounting and finance fields.

The Benefits Of Journaling

"

"

The Benefits of Journaling

Overcoming a painful past usually involves sharing one's story and the associated feelings. Developing insight into past hurts, and connecting the dots between then and now enables one to make better choices moving forward. Journal writing is a powerful tool that opens the path to greater insight and self-knowledge.

Journaling opens the door for the writer to express personal impressions, daily experiences, and evolving insights as well as reflections about the self, relationships, experiences, dreams, fantasies, and creative musings. This can be done without judgment or restriction. Reviewing earlier entries cultivates the writer's ability to learn from past events and circumstances that might otherwise go unnoticed. A repetitive, self-destructive behavior becomes more apparent when seen through the lens of these journal entries.

A Vehicle for Mindfulness

Journal writing can be a vehicle for deepening mindfulness as it helps to clarify and refine thoughts and emotions and brings the writer into the present. Like meditation, journal writing helps to clear the mind by transcribing emotional clutter onto the written page.

As the writer you get to become a witness to your past behaviors which then paves the way for fresh thoughts and perspectives. Journaling provides a forum that can be both cathartic (emotionally healing) and significant to understanding all the "Why" questions you might have.

A journal creates a great companion wherever you go. It is a resource for observing shifts in your inner world and outer behavior.

Keeping a journal is a great way to track your thoughts and feelings over time, but research and experience have shown that journaling has far-reaching benefits. In fact, journaling can affect virtually every aspect of your life, letting you better achieve success both personally and professionally. For solopreneurs and coaches, in particular, journaling can be an indispensable tool.

Developing a Habit

Fortunately, journaling doesn't have to take too much time; if you have five to 10 minutes to set aside each day, you'll be able to start the process and reap the benefits. While you might have some false starts along the way, making a commitment to maintaining your journal will ensure you're on the road to success, and, like any habit, consistency will pay off over time.

In addition to helping you add some structure to your life, which is especially useful for people with hectic lives, a journal can help you develop other healthy habits.
Your journal represents the point where you turn thoughts

in your mind into concrete ideas you can act on, and many people find it to be a centerpiece for achieving their goals both large and small.

The first step for deciding which type of journaling is best for you is deciding between a handwritten journal and a digital one. Handwriting your journal is the more traditional approach, letting you follow in the footsteps of thousands of years of tradition. Digital journaling, on the other hand, offers a certain level of convenience and access to a number of useful tools.

Deciding which is right for you is a personal decision, but it's worth noting that both are viable options worth consideration. Note that you don't have to focus exclusively on one type of journaling. Feel free to change which journaling methods you use over time and consider using digital and handwritten techniques for different types of journals.

For something so simple, there are an amazing number of benefits linked to journaling. These benefits are both subjective (personally felt) and objective (scientifically proven). As a mental health professional, I can attest to journaling working as I personally use it and recommend to all my clients.

Let's talk about the benefits of journaling because our brain always wants to know "Why".

11 Benefits of Journaling

Knowing Who You are: Understanding Your Personality And Identity

The many benefits of journaling:

- **Strengthens your immune system** and leads to better physical health

- **Improves emotional intelligence** (the ability to perceive and understand emotions)

- **Soothes anxiety** and increases feelings of calmness.

- **Promotes individuation** (the maturing of the self/identity)

- **Enhances mental health**

- **Helps you to deal better with depression)**

- **Encourages spiritual growth** and integration.

- **Reduces symptoms related to panic, PTSD, and addiction**

- **Increased self-awareness,** self-understanding, and self-compassion

- **Improves your ability to communicate** with others
- **Increases happiness**

- **Promotes mental clarity** and problem-solving skills

- **Helps you to deal with stress** and intrusive thoughts more effectively

- **Increases creativity**

- **Improves your work efficiency**

- **Can help to improve your IQ**

- **Speeds up emotional recovery** after romantic breakups

- **Promotes emotional, mental, physical, and spiritual healing**

I'm sure there are many other benefits I haven't mentioned here. For something so basic, this list shows a stunning array of benefits which virtually anyone can receive! All we need to do is learn how to make journaling a daily practice.

I hope this course will encourage to do more journaling and turn it into a **habit.**

If you want to continue journaling– here are some of my best tips:

1. Don't worry about the where..

Many people wonder whether paper diaries or digital diaries are better. My response is that none of them are superior: it all depends on the person. If you like to think over your thoughts and go slowly, writing in a traditional paper journal might be the best for you.

However, if you prefer the convenience of typing and if you like to move quickly with your thoughts, you might like to try an online journal or note-taking app such as Evernote, Microsoft OneNote, Penzu or another password secure website. Try exploring both and see what you like better. I prefer and recommend traditional pen and paper, see what works for you.

2. Keep your journal private

Your journal should be for your eyes only – it isn't to be shared on your Facebook page, Instagram account, YouTube channel, or other social media platform. It shouldn't even be shared with your friends, partner, or family members. Why? Because when we share thoughts and feelings with others, we tend to screen them for acceptability.

Your journal should be a place where you can write freely without the fear of judgment or scrutiny – therefore it's better to keep it private. No one is saying that you can't share some of your private reflections verbally with others, but just try to keep what you have written to yourself.

3. Don't bother with spelling, grammar, and punctuation

This is probably harder for perfectionist, who might have difficulty with grammatical and spelling errors. it can be hard to just let go. So here is why it is important to not bother about spelling, grammar, and punctuation: editing your journal entries actually stops your flow of thoughts and feelings because your focus will be more focused on trying to "play by the rules." Try to avoid being anal-retentive about writing: just let it all out – it feels so much better and Frees you

4. Forget about being a "good writer"

The purpose of journaling isn't to write a literary masterpiece, it is to self-reflect and record the thoughts and feelings you've been having for self-growth. Simply write whatever comes to mind and don't worry about whether it sounds poetic or eloquent.

5. Set a regular time of day

Making journaling into a habit requires you to set aside time every day. I like to personally write at the end of the day, but you might be different. Pick one period of the day and try to stick to it. For example, you might like to write first thing in the morning, after morning tea, after lunch time, or last thing at night. If you feel inspired to write at a time of the day you're not accustomed to writing, just flow with it. There are no set-in-stone rules here.

6. Write your deepest thoughts and feelings using the prompts in each lesson

Journaling is an intuitive activity because it requires you to tune into your feelings and blurt all of that out on paper. Sometimes I will write for a minute, and at other times I will write for up to an hour: it all depends on how I am feeling. So don't be afraid to delve deeply into your mind and heart beyond the prompts.

7. There's no need for time restrictions

Try to avoid setting rigid time limits: it's best just to allow your writing to flow. Of course, in an ideal world, we'd all have plenty of time to journal, but that's often not possible. So sometimes time restrictions are necessary (i.e. if you have an extremely busy life).

But if you have a bit of spare time, enjoy the feeling of letting your inner self materialize on paper. There's no need to "set aside ten minutes a day" as many people recommend – I find that time restrictions tend to make journaling into a chore rather than an enjoyable self-growth activity. But, as I said, if you have limited time available, time restrictions can come in handy.

8. If you're struggling, ask these questions ...

Sometimes we just don't feel "in the flow" of writing and sharing our thoughts doesn't come naturally. How am I feeling today? What is an issue I'm facing? What can I do about my most recent problem? What spiritual lesson is hidden in a difficult situation I'm facing? What thoughts are triggering my current feelings? Why do I keep having these thoughts?

What was the message hidden in last night's dream? What do I feel the need to change or improve about myself? (And why?) Am I being self-compassionate? Am I seeing the entire picture? How am I being dishonest with myself or others?   In what ways can I be more mindful? What mistaken beliefs am I buying into?   What is my plan of action to achieve my goals? What setbacks and obstacles am I facing?

These are only a few of the many potential questions you can ask yourself. I personally prefer to just allow my thoughts and feelings to flow– but other people prefer a more structured approach.

So if you're one of those people, you might like to keep a list of questions like the one above, close by.

9. Don't be afraid to explore traumatic experiences

Journaling is about growth, and growth often includes digesting past experiences. Sometimes the experiences we went through in the past were disturbing, traumatic or upsetting. Don't be afraid to explore these experiences – but just remember not to stay stuck in self-pity. It's OK to express your feelings loud and clear on paper; as it is a terrific form of catharsis.

But once you start ruminating and obsessing over these past experiences, then it's time to switch to your left hemisphere brain and start thinking about how you can overcome the pain inside of you practically.

10. Reflect on what you've written

After you've finished your journal entry, you might like to read back over what you've written with the intention of gaining clarity. As I mentioned previously, try not to nitpick your writing – spelling and all the rules of writing are irrelevant here.

What matters is that you gain a big picture perspective on how you think and feel. If any thoughts, feelings or realizations stand out to you, try highlighting them.

Reflection is what allows you to integrate your thoughts into knowledge, understanding, and inner transformation.

11. Write for the joy of it

Enjoy each day of journaling, find a place that makes you feel **"Ahhhhhhhhhh"** and begin to write...

In this book I give you prompts to help you enjoy these benefits and more.

You get to pick which section and which questions you wish to answer. I suggest investing minimum 5-10 minutes or 30 minutes a day. This whole book is a wholesale of Feel Good and Let Go prompts and questions to help you dig deeper into all aspects of life that make you who you truly are so that you can be free to be you, be free and be fearless when it comes to living your best life.

Happy Journaling !!

Journaling For

Self Discovery

Have you ever stopped to consider exactly what you want from life? Maybe you've taken this first step toward self-discovery, but haven't uncovered a path toward achieving your main goals.

Dreams, personal values, talents, even your personality traits may not always seem to matter much in the rush of daily life. But awareness of these characteristics can give you plenty of insight into your inner self.

Day-to-day priorities are important, certainly. But a life that's nothing more than a series of going through the same motions usually doesn't provide much enjoyment.

If you've reached a point in life where you find yourself asking, "Who am I, really?" some self-discovery can help you get to know yourself a little better.

Self-discovery might sound like a big, intimidating concept, but it's really just a process of:

- **examining your life**
- **figuring out what's missing**
- **taking steps toward fulfillment**

There's no better time for self-exploration than journaling, so here are some prompts to get you started.

Journal Prompts For Self Discovery

CHOOSE ONE PROMPT EACH DAY AND DEDICATE 5-10 MINUTES WRITING YOUR ANSWER. IF YOUR TIME RUNS LONGER BECAUSE YOU HAVE A LOT TO WRITE, SO BE IT. IF YOU CHOOSE MORE THAN ONE PROMPT SO BE IT....FREEDOM IS KEY.

1. Write 3 things you like about your appearance

2. What is your favorite thing about your personality?

3. What do you think your biggest weakness is? How can you work on improving this?

4. Who are you most grateful for having in your life?

5. Is there something you keep ruminating about that happened a long time ago?

6. How would your best friend describe you?

7. I am happiest when...

8.   What have you achieved that you are proud of?

9.   I feel peaceful when...

10. What is unique about your personality?

11. What goals are you working towards?

12. What are things that you need to stop doing that are making you unhappy?

13. What is your favorite thing to do to treat yourself?

14. When do you feel most confident?

15. What do your family love about you?

16. What is the last charitable thing you have done? If it was a long time ago, start now!

17. What parts of your life are you happy with?

18. How would your life change if you were confident?

19. Why do you think self-worth is important?

20. What is something you need to forgive yourself for?

21. What was the happiest time of your life? Why was that?

22. What traits do you admire in someone that you would like to have?

23. What parts of your life would you like to work on improving?

24. When was the last time you were kind to a stranger?

25. What habit do you need to stop?

26. What habit do you want to start for self-love?

27. What are your morals and values?

28. What negative beliefs do you hold about yourself?

29. What is something you want to do every day to build your confidence?

30. What do you think would make you happy?

31. What do you want to do more of in your life?

32. What is the nicest thing you have ever done for yourself?

33. What is the nicest compliment someone has ever given you?

34. What is something you need to let go of?

35. Why do you deserve to be happy?

36. What is something you are going to do that is nice for yourself today?

37. Write down 1 self-esteem goal for the future.

38. What compliment do you want the most? Give it to yourself.

39. Write down the positive ways you've changed over the past five or ten years.

40. Write a letter to yourself accepting yourself for who you are.

41. Write down ten positive affirmations that you can recite when you're overwhelmed by your insecurities.

42. What are 3 simple ways you can love yourself daily?

43. What's one thing you've done (no matter how small) that you're proud of yourself for?

44. Write down five positive things you can tell yourself instead of the typical negative self-talk.

45. What flaws and mistakes can you forgive yourself for?

46. What makes you feel loved?

47. What's a kind, level-headed way to respond when people make fun of you?

48. What sets your heart on fire, and why do you love yourself for that?

49. How can you make sure to fill your cup before giving yourself to others?

50. What do you feel like you need the most right now, and how can you meet that need?

51. If your closest friends were to write down your best personality traits, what would they be?

52. How can I meet my insecurities, mistakes, and flaws with grace, acceptance, and love today?

53. Picture all the people you feel judged by, and one by one write down why their opinions of you are wrong.

54. If you struggle with self-care, what are the top reasons you neglect taking care of yourself?

55. What's the first thing you turn to when you feel sad? Is it a healthy thing?

56. What are ten things you're grateful for?

57. Who's approval do you want the most, and why?

58. What hobbies did you have as a kid that you dropped? Why did you drop them?

59. You're at your happiest when you're . . .

60. What have you purposefully skipped out on, even if you wanted it? What stopped you?

61. What motivates you the most (fear, money, happiness, etc.)?

62. Write down a definition of who you are—the good and the bad.

63. What activities drain your energy the most?

64. What activities give you energy?

65. After spending time with someone, do you typically walk away feeling loved or judged?

66. Do you assume people judge/dislike you based on past experiences? How can you work through that?

67. What are your three biggest pet peeves?

68. What's your biggest insecurity?

69. Who inspires you the most and why?

70. If money wasn't an issue, how would you live the rest of your life?

71. What negative or traumatic experiences have you let define you, and how can you walk away from them?

72. What are you afraid of the most?

73. What things have you loved doing all of your life?

74. What thought patterns have you noticed lately, and are they healthy or toxic?

75. Where would you be if all of your goals were accomplished?

76. What goals have you let fall by the wayside?

77. Do your current goals align with your core values?

78. What would your highest self say to your current self?

79. What's a limiting perspective or mindset that you've lived with your entire life? How are you going to work through it?

80. Write down one good habit you want to start working on.

81. What are your biggest time wasters?

82. What changes do you want to see in your life in five years?

83. How can you brighten up your loved ones' days?

84. What do you want to be remembered for, and how can you work toward that?

85. How can you stay on top of your goals and New Year's resolutions?

86. What past experiences am I still healing from that I need to give myself grace for?

87. What dreams do you need to put on hold for right now so you can pursue your purpose?

88. What gets you out of bed in the morning? Are you pursuing that daily?

89. What things am I willing to let go of so I can live my best life?

90. What habits, memories, relationships, etc. are you holding onto that are keeping you from improving yourself?

91. What boundaries do you need to set with others and yourself to prioritize your goals and self care?

92. When do I feel most confident in myself, and when do I feel the least confident in myself?

93. What would your life look like if you were fully confident in yourself and your opinions? What steps can you take to get closer to that?

94. Allow yourself to think about what your ideal life would look like, and then write it all down.

95. LIVE LAUGH AND Enjoy A life that is yours and yours only. You get to create and live your best life.

96. I am grateful for...

97. I am craving...

98. I feel most like myself when...

99. Something I would love to do but not sure I can is...

100. I feel amazing about myself when I...

101. I feel negatively about myself when I...

102. I've been putting off...

103. I would love to get some support with...

104. I feel...

105. My biggest regret is...

106. My ideal day would look like...

107. One thing I've always wanted to try but haven't is...

108. To me, success looks like...

109. My biggest fear is...

110. My biggest strength is...

111. Over the next year, I would like to improve on...

112. The best piece of advice I've ever received is...

113. If I was speaking to younger self, I would tell them...

114. Right now, I feel like I am missing...

115. The most important people in my life are...

116. My biggest insecurity is...

117. The thing I love most about myself is...

118. I can't stand it when other people...

119. I feel most valued and loved when...

120. To someone I mistreated in the past, I would say...

121. My spiritual beliefs are...

122. My boundaries are...

123. My dream career is...

124. I feel most unsatisfied when...

125. I show my love for others by...

126. When I am challenged, I feel...

127. When somebody breaks my trust, I feel...

128. When I am struggling, I need...

129. Signs that I am overwhelmed are...

130. I feel most creative when...

131. When I feel unappreciated, I...

132. I am most productive when...

133. When I am feeling low, the best way to lift my mood is...

134. I feel most at home when...

135. My worst habit is...

136. My fondest memory is...

137. My worst memory is...

138. I couldn't imagine living without...

139. To me, love means...

140. Something I wish others knew about me is...

141. I feel healthiest when...

142. I would describe myself as...

143. My biggest life lesson has been...

144. Something I would love to learn more about is...

145. I feel happiest in my skin when...

146. In ten years, I see myself as...

147. To me, happiness means...

148. If I knew I couldn't fail, I would...

149. If I could go anywhere in the world, I would go...

150. The person I look up to most is...

151. I feel most at peace when...

152. I want to be seen/recognized as...

153. Something I need to let go of is...

154. I could take better care of myself by...

155. By the end of my life, I want to have accomplished...

156. I feel most alive when...

157. I feel most inspired by...

158. I manage stress by...

159. The best gift I've ever given or received is...

160. Something that excites me about the future is...

161. My relationship with social media is...

162. My favorite hobby is...

163. Something that has been bothering me recently is...

164. I could be calmer if I...

165. To me, the meaning of life is...

166. Something that makes me sad is...

167. I feel most anxious when...

168. I would like to feel...

169. Habits that support my wellbeing are...

170. I feel guilty when...

171. I feel connected to the universe/god when...

172. I feel most confident when...

173. I could enjoy my life more by...

174. I often get compliments about...

175. My favorite thing to do with other people is...

Journaling For

Letting Go

B efore I share the prompts for letting go, let me just explain a little about letting go.

Letting go does not mean allowing toxic people and behaviour to be present in your life all in the name of positivity, letting go and not holding onto grudges.

If you need to hold onto that grudge in order to protect yourself, you dig your nails in, girl. I stand by you.

What 'letting go' means in the context of this blog post is processing past events, healing from them, and ultimately not allowing them to negatively affect you anymore.

You can look back on them and either think about what you learned from that situation or simply brush it off as something that did once hurt you, but no longer does.

It might even still hurt you – and that's okay – but it no longer causes your heart to skip a beat or stomach to clench. **Letting go, especially of what doesn't serve you, is the ultimate way to grow as a human being as not only do you learn from it, you also release the negative feelings attached to it.**

This isn't to say you're not allowed to still acknowledge that a situation hurt you. In fact, pinpointing where and how you were hurt is how we build and enforce boundaries – a key element of self-care.

You just no longer let that situation haunt you.
The emotion you feel is dulled and you can disconnect from it whenever you need.

Here's an analogy for you, I do love analogies.

Imagine the specific situation or person you can't let go of as a dumbbell. A heavy weight.

Letting go is not burying your dumbbell under a pile of clothes, hiding it in a cupboard or giving it to someone else to carry; letting go is merely setting it down yourself and walking away from it, free to live your life.

It still exists, it's still there, and you know that. Sometimes you might even have to pick it up to move some other stuff around and tidy up some other mess.

But you're no longer burdened by the weight of it all day, every day.

Learning to let go of past experiences has definitely helped me process emotions and move on in a positive, healthy way that ultimately benefits me.

It's helped me stop over-thinking every little mistake I

made in the past or every bad thing that anyone has ever done to me.

(Although I have never forgotten or forgiven the people that did said bad things to me. They're still not in my life. I know my worth and I'm firm with my boundaries.)

This has helped with my feeling of inner peace and improved my mindset overall as I'm not always dwelling on the past.

However, I do want to reiterate that letting go does not mean forgiveness or forgetting.
If someone hurt you, you absolutely shouldn't feel obligated to forgive them or let them back in your life.

When people show you who they are, BELIEVE them. Protect your energy.

It just means not being obsessed or preoccupied with that person and whatever they did to you for the rest of time.
It means processing and healing from it.
Letting go and moving on from what no longer serves you can be good for you in a few ways.

- Improve your outlook and mindset in general as you no longer feel angry or bitter (even though those feelings are probably valid and justified)

- Boost self-esteem as you feel powerful for rising

above the situation and moving on

- Stop over-thinking, which tends to also help you sleep better as an added bonus

- Relieves anxiety and improves mental health

- Improves relationships and communication

- Helps you set and enforce clear boundaries

- Protects your energy

- Makes you better at processing and healing from negative emotions in a healthy way

- Teaches you healthy coping strategies

- Gives you more time for positive stuff

Ultimately, while not essential for happiness, letting go can really help with healing and growth as a person.

WHEN SHOULD YOU USE JOURNAL PROMPTS FOR LETTING GO?

If you're really struggling to move on from something like a failed relationship, argument with a family member, or betrayal from a close friend, journal prompts for letting go can help you process and move on from the situation.

They can help put the situation into perspective so that you can make a decision – if there's a decision to be made that is – and heal.

You can then move forward with your life, taking only what serves you from it (i.e. a lesson, boundaries, e.t.c.).

When it comes to moving on from past traumatic events, while journal prompts for letting go can be helpful, I would also strongly advise you see a therapist who's got plenty of experience in this area.

Huge traumatic events need to be handled in a specific way that you may need professional help to deal with. This isn't to say that the life events I mentioned above, such as break-ups and family fall-outs can't be traumatic.

If you're struggling to get over any life event that has impacted your mental health, I want to encourage you to seek professional help.
If you want to improve your mindset, I'd also recommend:

- Meditation and mindfulness
- Shadow work
- Self-care
- Goal/intention setting
- Practicing gratitude
- Repeat affirmations
- Finding a creative outlet

Journal Prompts For Letting Go

CHOOSE ONE PROMPT EACH DAY AND DEDICATE 5-10 MINUTES WRITING YOUR ANSWER. IF YOUR TIME RUNS LONGER BECAUSE YOU HAVE A LOT TO WRITE, SO BE IT. IF YOU CHOOSE MORE THAN ONE PROMPT SO BE IT....FREEDOM IS KEY.

HERE ARE THE JOURNAL PROMPTS FOR LETTING GO AND MOVING ON

1. Does this [insert person, situation, or memory of an event] serve me anymore? If yes, how so?

2. Why am I finding it so hard to move on from this?

3. What emotions does this event or memory trigger in me?

4. Has this affected other areas of my life? How so?

5. Has this affected how I treat others or approach situations? How so?

6. What makes me feel safe?

7. What would I gain by letting go? How would it make me feel?

8. What are three things I can do right now to make me feel better?

9. What are three long-term things I can do to move on from this and heal?

10. What triggers me to over-think?

11. What's one event I lose sleep over?

12. "Other people's opinions of you are none of your business." How does this statement make you feel? Why?

13. Why do I choose to dwell on things I can't control or change? Where does this come from?

14. Write about a tough situation you've overcome.

15. Write about your five strongest traits.

16. What are five things that make you happy?

17. I'm okay with not having all the answers because...

18. What does 'letting go' really mean for me?

19. I choose to put my energy into what serves me. This includes...

20. How have I grown from my past struggles and experiences?

Please know that Letting go takes time.

It's really important that you're gentle and kind to yourself during this process.

You won't suddenly let go of something that's been haunting you for years just because you've written about it a couple of times. It takes patience and work.

Allow yourself to feel to heal and I invite you to do some shadow work. It's really helped me.

You'll get there. And you'll be so much stronger for it.

Journaling For

Self-Care

Journaling For Self-Care

The benefits of journaling for self-care include:

- Reduced stress
- Improved mental clarity
- Increased self-awareness
- Strengthened emotional maturity
- Reduced disagreements with others
- Improved focus
- More peace of mind
- Less anxiety
- Improved memory

To cover self-care, I want to relay to you again why journaling in itself is self-care and the many benefits that we take for granted. Journaling helps you get to know yourself. You create your own log of what sparks certain emotions, how you consistently think of yourself, what parts of your life you are grateful for, and what you feel you need to change to change. Journaling can make you more aware of your emotional cycles.

Journaling can help you answer questions about yourself and help you become more conscious. Journaling provides a private and accessible way to notice the things that make you happy, anxious, or content. When you have access to more data or evidence of your emotions, you're able to make improvements to your life in a more guided and focused manner.

Journaling looks different for everyone. Each person has different goals for mindfulness, self-care, and improving themselves, so Please, please don't worry about comparing the way you journal to the ways other people journal.

Depending on your lifestyle, it may be easier to jot down short phrases or sentences throughout the day, or you might want to devote fifteen minutes before bed. Many people who practice journaling to improve their mindfulness like freewriting for a set amount of time in the morning to start the day off on a good note.

Before you try journaling for mindfulness and self-care, you should define your goal or purpose for journaling, set the intention.

What are you hoping to get out of this habit? Knowing this before you start can serve as a guidepost for the types of things you may focus on writing about, and it'll serve as a useful benchmark in the future to look back on.

Whether you're looking to start journaling to understand your emotions better, understand the things in your life that trigger negative reactions or you want memories to look back on, it's good to know where you're starting.

Taking note of what you want to get out of journaling is extremely useful for measuring how journaling can improve your life.

After figuring out why you want to journal, the next step is to gather the tools and materials you'll need to make the habit stick. Set goals for how much or how long you'll write while you build up the habit.

Whether it's for 10, 15, 30 minutes before bed or at least three sentences a day, choose a goal that you can achieve each day easily.

Ensure journaling feels like a retreat, not a responsibility.

If a nice pen and a nice journal inspire you to write a bit each day, choose inviting materials that make you excited to write a little bit down each day. I'm personally a huge notebook junkie and can't resist a pretty, functional notebook.

Self-care is the practice of fulfilling your needs and dedicating time to practices that help you feel healthy and safe.

Improving your mindfulness is one act of self-care, and journaling is a proven way to help you improve your mental clarity and take care of your mind and body.

Ways to use journaling for self-care include:

- Releasing built up emotions
- Building emotional vocabulary
- Create more peace of mind
- Discovering more about yourself
- Creating a self-care ritual with some restorative "me time"

Journaling can provide an outlet for emotions that you want to get out healthily and privately.

Writing out your feelings can also help you feel more in control of how you express yourself.

Simply naming your feelings helps calm them, a phenomenon called "name it to tame it"

This mindful way of expressing your feelings creates less opportunity for emotions to build up to a boiling point and cause you to react or act in ways you know aren't as productive or as healthy as if you were to a journal.

Improved emotional vocabulary from journaling is a form of self-care as it can help you feel more empowered in the way you express your emotions. You can become more confident in expressing and communicating your feelings from journaling consistently.

Journaling for self-care can easily turn into journaling for self-discovery. This can be used as a tool to help you improve your life by understanding you triggers, patterns, and even past traumas that are ready for healing.

Lastly, creating a mindful ritual around your journaling is a useful form of self-care as well.

You might want to make a cup of your favorite tea, grab a pen that makes you feel fabulous, light a candle, burn incense, or play a favorite song while you journal.

WHAT TO WRITE IN YOUR SELF-CARE JOURNAL

If when you decide to write you grab your journal and a pen, open the page and your mind goes blank. Don't worry.

This happens to almost anyone who has ever tried to journal and that is why I have prompts in all sections which cover self-care if you feel stuck.

You grab your journal and a pen, open the page and your mind goes blank. Don't worry. This happens to almost anyone who has ever tried to journal.

The following are some ways you may choose to write your self-care journaling:

FREE WRITING

Open up to a blank page and write whatever comes to mind. Don't censor or delete anything. Even starting with "I don't know what to write" is a perfect way to begin. Write down what you think at that moment you open the page or write down how you feel. Let the words flow from your brain to the page.

You can free-write for a specific amount of time or until you fill up half a page. Once you've met your goal for the free write, you can stop right there. But if you find you have more to put on the page after the timer goes off, keep writing until you feel content.

WRITE IN A LIST FORMAT

If you don't want to write full sentences, a gratitude list is a helpful format to test out. You can also write a short list, such as three things you're looking forward to that day, and then write a short paragraph to go along with the shortlist.

Or, if you're feeling inspired to write a longer list, you can write a list of your most favorite memories or a list of the characteristics you like most about yourself. Whatever the topic is, make sure it encourages you to reflect on yourself, your emotions, or your goals.

ANSWER OR RESPOND TO PREVIOUS ENTRIES

If you've been journaling for a while but are feeling stuck on a new entry, try reading through past entries you've made and write a short reflection.

How have you changed? Do you still feel or think the way you did when you wrote on a previous day?

These reflection entries can help you look back at what struggles are sticking with you and what your life changes have been beneficial. Reading through and creating a new entry responding to your previous journaling pages is a great way to see your evolution.

WRITE ABOUT YOUR GOALS

Not only does journaling encourage self-reflection, but it can also help you look forward and think about your future goals. Imagine what you want your life to be like and write that down. You can be as creative or straightforward as you like.

Since your journal is private, you can write down whatever you like without having to worry about how it will come off to someone else. **Journaling is the time for you to be alone with your thoughts.**

Writing down your goals can help you keep track of what you desire in life. When you journal about your goals, it's your opportunity to put them into action. Acknowledging to yourself what you want is the first step to achieving it. Journaling is the perfect place to feel comfortable and safe, acknowledging the goals you have for yourself.

MAKE IT CATHARTIC

Not only can you journal in ways that help you be self-reflective and think about your goals, but you can also journal about the things you want to let go of or move on from.

MAKE IT SELF REFLECTIVE

Not only can you journal in ways that help you be self-reflective and think about your goals, but you

can also journal about the things you want to let go
of or move on from.

If you want to release emotions or thoughts, you feel the
need to communicate, but you don't feel comfortable
sharing them with someone else, journaling, and then
throwing away the page can be useful.

**If you have negative emotions or thoughts that you
feel the need to put into words, you don't have to
save the entry.** Simply writing the thoughts down is a
release. You can tear out the page after writing and throw it
away. You can even rip it up if that helps you feel better.
Writing to release your emotions has been used as a healthy
coping mechanism for many people.

You don't have to do this with every journal entry, but if
there are ones, you're compelled to get rid of, it may help
you feel a healthy sense of relief if there are emotions you
want to let go of and move on from.

**Journaling to release emotions and thoughts is a
wonderful element to incorporate into of a full
moon practice for self-care.**

BULLET JOURNALING

You can actually use any of the other suggestions in your bullet journal instead of a traditional lined journal, but I wanted to point it out separately. Bullet journaling is usually done on a blank page or a page with grid dot guides.

Bullet journaling for self-care can offer additional benefits because people usually decorate their bullet journal pages. The space to doodle, draw, paint, or place your favorite stickers gives you the chance to express yourself creatively and release even more stress. One study found that even simple drawing like creating stick figures reduces stress-related hormones in your body. Wow! The beauty of writing and coloring.

Hope this helps to get you started. Please make time for self -care.

Happy Journaling. Be Encouraged

Journal Prompts For Self-Care

CHOOSE ONE PROMPT EACH DAY AND DEDICATE 5-10 MINUTES WRITING YOUR ANSWER. IF YOUR TIME RUNS LONGER BECAUSE YOU HAVE A LOT TO WRITE, SO BE IT. IF YOU CHOOSE MORE THAN ONE PROMPT SO BE IT....FREEDOM IS KEY.

1. Write the good parts of your day

It doesn't hurt to start your self-care journal off on a positive note. You can start it off that way by writing down the good parts of your day. Did you have a good time with someone today? Did you enjoy a great workout? Was there something new you learned that inspired you?

Write these or any other good moment that happened in your day. In a way, you'll be reliving those good feelings again.

2. Write the bad parts of your day

There are good parts of our days, and then of course there are also bad parts. Sometimes they can stay in your mind all day, weighing you down with negative emotions.

When you're writing in your journal, this can be your time to let out all of those bad moments that happened. Talk about how you felt in that moment, what you wish would have happened differently. Letting out all of the emotion of the bad parts of your day can be a way to give yourself a good release.

You may feel less weighed down by those emotions after you write them down.

3. Note what you were thinking about today

We think a lot of different thoughts in our days. Sometimes we're dwelling over a major life decision that we're considering. Other times we may be thinking about moments in our past that continue to come up in our thoughts.

Other times spouse, children are just hitting the wrong nerves.

Talk about how you felt in whatever moment comes to light, what you wish would have happened differently. Letting out all of the emotion of the bad parts of your day can be a way to give yourself a good release.

You may feel less weighed down by those emotions after you write them down. Remember this is what you wish could have happened, try not to put too much emphasis on what the other person or people could have done as you don't have control over what others do or how they react.

4. Write answers to why

It can sometimes help to go a little bit deeper into your thoughts and feelings. Ask yourself why you're thinking and feeling certain things.

Why are you feeling certain insecurities in your life currently? Why are you struggling with certain emotions right now?

When you try to answer those "why" questions, you might find it helps you get to a deeper understanding about yourself.

Maybe it leads you to some past issues you need to heal from. I like this idea that there's usually something deeper behind the frustrations we often feel in life.

5. Make a gratitude list

A gratitude list can be particularly great for the bad days you have in life. No matter how bad your day may have been, it's always possible you can find something to be grateful for. I try to write at least 5-10 things I am grateful for a day.

6. Write positive memories

When we find our minds going back to the past, so often our mind goes towards the negative. That one bad moment we've never been able to just forget about. Things we wish we would have done if we could go back in time.

You can use your journal to re-shift your focus when it comes to your past. Life may not be turning out exactly the way you planned, but there's still a lot of good that's happened anyway.

Take time to reflect on some of the most positive moments in your life. Maybe it'll inspire you to re-create those positive moments again.

At the very least, it'll help you be more kind to yourself about acknowledging you've given yourself some pretty good moments in life.

7. Keep a list of your favorite activities

Making a list of your favorite activities should be an essential part of your journaling for self-care. When you need to give yourself day of self-care, you can go to this list of favorite activities, and schedule them in your day.

It'll save you the time of having to think about what to do for yourself. Some examples of self-care activities you might enjoy including having a nice bubble bath, enjoying a walk in nature, or doing something creative

You can continually add to this list, so you have a variety of options to consider when you need some self-care in your day.

8. Keep a list of your favorite meals

Sometimes a delicious meal can be a way to give ourselves a nice boost in our day. You can write down a list of some of your favorite meals that you enjoy.

When you need that boost, you can look to your journal to pick out one of those meals you can make or buy. Preferably, it's helpful if these meals are ones that are good for you too.

You can continually add to this list, so you have a variety of options to consider when you need some self-care in your day.

9. Make a goal list

Another useful journaling tip is to make a goal list. Don't just write the goals down, but also decide that you're going to try to do one thing every day that gets you closer to that goal.

You can write down what you did in your day that was your one step towards your goal. It can be a great way to keep yourself motivated.

10. Write down your hopes for the future

What is your dream future, what would you like to see happen in your life, family's life?

One best way of writing this part is through affirmations of your hopes and dreams for the future. I do have a companion book to this which covers Affirmations for all aspects of life, business and more.

In that book I have a whole section on **DREAM LIFE JOURNALING** and Affirmations that go with creating a dream life.

Journaling For

Burnout

B urnout is sneaky and can truly go unnoticed for a very long time. It can catch you off guard when you least expect it. Many times, the warning signs are there. If you are super ambitious, you may softly "poo-poo" the red flags away.

Thinking of the end goal of a project is much more gratifying than the need to stop and rejuvenate. Trust me I know. I ended up having diabetes and that was how I slowed down.

Burnout can really cramp your ability to pursue your goals, especially if self-care is neglected. Because burnout is a gradual process, being on the lookout for the warning signs -- physical, behavioral, and emotional -- is important.

Fill your paper with the breathings of your heart." — William Wordsworth

PHYSICAL SIGNS OF BURNOUT:
- Feeling worn-out most of the time
- Shifting appetite and sleep habits from the normal routine
- Weakening immune system

EMOTIONAL SIGNS OF BURNOUT:
- Motivation tanks
- Increasingly critical and negative
- Feeling caged in, helpless, and defeated
- What once brought joy is no longer fulfilling

BEHAVIOR SIGNS OF BURNOUT:

- Spending more time alone
- Procrastinating
- Taking out your frustrations on others
- Using food, alcohol and drugs to cope

One way to process what you are feeling is to get it out of your head and down on paper. Journaling for burnout self-care can be an aid. Perhaps you haven't noticed any symptoms, but by writing down your feelings you may find a pattern that you would not have noticed if you didn't see it visually.

The journaling prompts below can help you get into the habit of writing for self-care and will guide you in a direction you may not have ever thought of on your own.

The prompts are designed to help you explore your thoughts and feelings. There is no wrong or right way to pen your thoughts. Let whatever comes to mind when you read the prompt flow onto the paper and see where it takes you. Maybe the word or phrase reminds you of a specific memory or feeling.

Allow yourself to write about that memory or explore the emotion. Do not be concerned with grammar or mechanics. Try not to edit your thoughts (or writing) and instead give yourself permission to freely write without judgement.

Journal Prompts For Burnout

CHOOSE ONE PROMPT EACH DAY AND DEDICATE 5-10 MINUTES WRITING YOUR ANSWER. IF YOUR TIME RUNS LONGER BECAUSE YOU HAVE A LOT TO WRITE, SO BE IT. IF YOU CHOOSE MORE THAN ONE PROMPT SO BE IT....FREEDOM IS KEY.

"Write hard and clear about what hurts."
— Ernest Hemingway

1. I find myself repeating this script in my head today:_____

2. Right now, I feel challenged by _____. I feel supported when _____.

3. I have been paying a lot of attention to _____. I would like to pay more attention to _____; I can devote more energy to the better-feeling alternatives by _____.

67

4. The things that help me the most right now are..._____

5. What can I do *in this moment* to get myself some nourishment and self-care?

6. I am thankful that I..._____

7. How might this stressful experience transform me into a more loving (compassionate, forgiving, patient, helpful, or faithful) person?

8. What past challenge has turned out to be a gift in disguise (even if it's still painful)? Why? What was the silver lining?

9. What's not wrong in my life? Here are three things that I can think of right now:

10. If I knew that anything I asked for would be answered, I would ask for _____.

11. What do I want my life to FEEL like?

12. How do you shift your mindset if it isn't working for you?

13. How do you recharge?

14. How can you celebrate yourself today?

15. What does your situational best look like today?

16. What helps you slow down and feel more present?

17. What can you do today that you didn't think you could do a year ago?

18. What's a goal you want to accomplish and why?

19. How do you put yourself first without feeling guilty?

20. How do you practice self-acceptance?

21. How do you stay focused and steer clear of distractions?

22. How do you trust yourself to make big decisions?

23. How do you set boundaries and avoid absorbing someone else's emotions and stress?

24. How do you savor the time you get alone?

25. How do you notice when you're nearing burnout?

26. How do you share your feelings with the people who care about you?

27. How do you swap envy for joy when other people accomplish things?

28. How do you advocate for yourself?

29. How do you forgive yourself when you make a mistake?

30. How do you ask for help or support when you need it?

31. How do you practice self-love and self-kindness?

32. How do you calm your nerves in a difficult situation?

33. How do you make the time you spend with people more intentional?

34. How do you embrace your authentic self, even if it looks different from what others expect?

35. How do you set and protect your boundaries?

36. What new opportunities have come out of challenges you've faced?

37. How can you step outside your comfort zone to grow?

38. How do you remind yourself that you're enough?

"Tears are words that need to be written."
— *Paulo Coelho*

Journaling For

The
Workplace

Journal Prompts For The Workplace

CHOOSE ONE PROMPT EACH DAY AND DEDICATE 5-10 MINUTES WRITING YOUR ANSWER. IF YOUR TIME RUNS LONGER BECAUSE YOU HAVE A LOT TO WRITE, SO BE IT. IF YOU CHOOSE MORE THAN ONE PROMPT SO BE IT....FREEDOM IS KEY.

1. What goals do I want to achieve this quarter? How will I achieve those goals?

2. What did I learn today?

3. What could I have done better this week?

4. What is my biggest issue in terms of organization and time management?

5. How can I be a better communicator?

6. What did I do today that will get me closer to my career goals?

7. I am proud of myself professionally because
_____.

8. What is it about my job that makes me happiest?

9. What is one area I can learn more about in order to be better at my job?

10. What is the next step in my career, and can that be done in my current position? If not, what is my plan? If so, how will I manifest that?

11. What are my biggest weaknesses professionally? How can I turn those into strengths or at least less problematic weaknesses?

12. What are my strengths? Am I putting those strengths to good use?

13. What mistakes did I make this week and what did I learn from them?

14. How am I spending my time on a daily basis? Is there anything that needs to be adjusted?

15. What am I most proud of professionally? Why?

16. Is there professional development or educational training I need/want to pursue to improve and further my career? How can I make that a reality?

17. What do I want my career to look like in one year? What are my action steps?

18. What do I want my career to look like in five years? 10 years? What are my action steps?

19. Does my job leave me feeling professionally fulfilled? Does it make me happy? Why or why not?

20. What is my ideal work routine? How can I make that a reality in my life?

21. What is one lesson (or lessons, if you have many!) that I learned today?

22. Did anyone compliment or comment my work today? What did they say?

23. What is one big thing that I accomplished today? Did I do anything above and beyond my basic job description today?

24. What is one way that I can go above and beyond tomorrow?

25. What could I have done to be more productive?

26. What was something proactive I did today?

27. What is a gap in the business that I could solve? What could I do?

28. What task was the most energizing? What was the most draining?

29. What am I grateful for at work?

30. What are three things I have to accomplish tomorrow?

31. What were some internal and external challenges?

32. What are some personal and professional development activities I've done? (Such as classes, networking events, informational interviews, reading industry publications.)

33. Who did I reach out to and connect with?

34. What are my short-term and long-term goals?

35. How did I help my colleagues or clients?

36. What do I like or dislike about the company culture?

"

Journaling For

Business Owners

"

Powerful Journal Prompts for Business Owners

If you're anything like me, you like the idea of planning, getting organized, and setting goals. But once you get out of dreaming mode and start doing? There can be a big disconnect. What has helped me in my business is journaling.

How I started my daily business journaling practice

- **I started with assigning my patients to answer journal prompts relating to our sessions and for years many patients reported the benefits of having the prompts to guide them. I started gathering the prompts and making them into pdf booklets to give to my patients. I then started answering the same questions for myself.**

Now I can keep journals everywhere for everything

- **I added to my To DO LIST** – I treat my journaling as a non-negotiable just like I do walking as a form of exercise everyday.

- **I got clear on my goals for journaling.** I want to level up my mindset, practice visualization, and use journaling as a way to increase my self-trust as I do the often-uncomfortable work (in that "edge of my comfort zone!" way) of growing my business.

- **I chose journal prompts that would support those goals.** I looked for prompts that would help me visualize success, and feel positive. I also looked for prompts that would help me see my blind spots as an online business owner who's in a season of growing her business.

- **I keep it short:** I love that saying KISS Keep it simple stupid... not in that sense but I am learning short is sweet.

- **I now look for prompts that remind me to take care of myself, as a business, because my business is all me.**

What I do at the start and end of my workday:

- I start each work session by responding to journal prompts for about 15 minutes.

- I don't do this in my normal workspace. I intentionally go to another place in my home or workspace that feels comfortable and relaxed – and that isn't directly in front of my computer.

- I try not to judge myself about what comes up. I focus on looking at exactly where I am in the moment and considering what I can do to take care of myself.

This practice has dramatically increased my self-compassion. It's definitely changed how I feel about what I accomplish every day. It's created a hard stop to the end of my workday, which can be challenging to find as someone who is self-employed!

I've found that ending the day in self-reflection has helped me to feel significantly better. I don't end the day in a rush anymore, or by telling myself I didn't get enough done, because I've created space to counter those automatic negative thoughts.

And when you work for yourself, and the work is literally never done? The pride and relief of finishing on a contemplative note – even if I didn't accomplish my whole list – feels incredible!

Would you like to join me?

Here are the prompts that I'm using to coach myself daily: Here are the prompts I use:

Powerful Entrepreneur/Business Owners Journal Prompts

1. What do I need to hear today?

2. What does my body need today?

3. If my only job was to take care of my needs, what would I need right now? Physically? Emotionally? Energetically?

4. When did I feel most in your element today?

5. What am I most proud of yourself for doing, regardless of the outcome?

6. What can you do to make it easy to feel motivated today?

7. What are 15 things that you're grateful for in my life today?

8. What are 15 things that you're grateful for in my business today?

9. How do I want to feel? What thoughts would create that?

10. What did I avoid today?

11. Where am I indulging in confusion or overwhelm, instead of making a decision?

12. Am I confused and overwhelmed, or am I tired? hungry?

13. When did I hear my intuition today?

14. What do I believe I need to do next?

15. Do my thoughts about what I need to do next support my needs? My health? Do they expand my choices? Do they make me feel empowered? If not, what else are my options?

16. If I was going to practice deeply believing myself today, what would I give myself permission to do?

17. What am I getting from this situation?

18. If I was my bravest self today, what would I be doing?

19. What's the first step in the right direction?

20. What could I do less of?

From Below Choose one prompt per day (perhaps put them on slips of paper and draw one at random!), and then write non-stop for at least 10 minutes.

The longer you write, the deeper you'll dive and the more surprised you'll be by what you uncover.

This process is sure to help you grow as a small business owner—and as a person.

Have some fun!

Journal Prompts For Business Owners

CHOOSE ONE PROMPT EACH DAY AND DEDICATE 5-10 MINUTES WRITING YOUR ANSWER. IF YOUR TIME RUNS LONGER BECAUSE YOU HAVE A LOT TO WRITE, SO BE IT. IF YOU CHOOSE MORE THAN ONE PROMPT SO BE IT....FREEDOM IS KEY.

1. 20 things that make me smile

2. What I wish others knew about me

3. How do I want people to feel when they first encounter my brand?

4. If I could be exactly as I wanted, I'd...

5. You are writing a book. What will it be called? What will it be about?

6. I feel most successful when...

7. A big step I've been thinking about for far too long...

8. How I recently stretched beyond my comfort zone & what I learned

9. If I could meet any fictional character, it would be ... because...

10. The time I laughed the hardest was...

11. My 15-year-old self would be proud of me today for...

12. Someone whose life is better because of me (and why)...

13. I secretly wish I...

14. If I were a superhero, my special power would be...

15. When people first meet me, I hope they feel...

16. My favorite quote and why I love it

17. If my best friend or spouse described me, what would they say?

18. What would a stranger say?

19. What does happiness mean to me?

20. What advice would I give to my teenage self?

21. What sets my soul on fire?

22. What would I do if I couldn't fail?

23. What is my favorite childhood memory?

24. What do I want my legacy to be?

25. If money were no object, what would I do?

26. When people first meet me, how do I want them to feel?

Journaling For

Pursuing Success

Journal Prompts For Pursuing Success

CHOOSE ONE PROMPT EACH DAY AND DEDICATE 5-10 MINUTES WRITING YOUR ANSWER. IF YOUR TIME RUNS LONGER BECAUSE YOU HAVE A LOT TO WRITE, SO BE IT. IF YOU CHOOSE MORE THAN ONE PROMPT SO BE IT....FREEDOM IS KEY.

When it comes to journaling for success the question that arises frequently is, "What do I write?" The true answer -- "Anything you want" -- isn't particularly helpful for someone feeling stuck. So here are 50 prompts to get your ideas flowing. In typical coaching form, I present them as questions on which you can reflect and record.

1. What is your definition of success right now?

2. How does success look to you 5 years from now?

3. What actions can you take to meet your goals today, this week, this month?

87

4. How much do you believe in yourself and why?

5. What kind of support network do you have to support your goals?

6. What messages about success did you get growing up?

7. Who or what shaped your ideas of success?

8. How flexible are your plans for success? How detailed are they? And how important are they?

9. What do you tell yourself about success?

10. And what do the people around you and society say?

11. Do you think you deserve success? Why or why not?

12. How will you feel once you reach success?

13. What successes have you already experienced in your life?

14. List all your strengths and how you can use them to build success.

15. How can you work around your weaknesses?

16. What message do you want to send to the world with your success?

17. What do you need to heal or what needs fixing first to become successful? (Maybe nothing, but it's good to know.)

18. Name 10 emotions tied to the word "success".

19. What are your hobbies and interests, and how can they fuel your success?

20. How committed to success are you?

21. What excites you the most about having success?

22. What will you do with your success when you reach it?

23. Write out a 5 year plan for your success.

24. Describe how hard work is connected to success and how you feel about working hard for success.

25. How can you improve your outcomes for success?

26. If I was guaranteed unlimited time and money, with the only condition being that I pursue my dream career, what would I do?

27. What did I particularly enjoy doing as a child?

28. Who are the 3-5 people I admire most in the world? What do I admire about them?

29. What activities light me up, energize me, or make me feel stronger, better, or more inspired?

30. If I were granted an extra hour each day, and all basic needs (i.e., sleep) were met, how would I spend it?

31. Who is living a courageous life? Why do they come to mind? What can I learn from their experience?

32. If I am completely honest with myself, what beliefs or assumptions hold me back?

33. What's the best job I've ever had? What made it so great?

34. Who would I want giving toasts about my life at my 95th birthday party? What would I want them to say?

35. Who in my world inspires me? What do I learn from them?

36. What's the best book I've ever read and/or movie I've ever watched? What stands out about them?

37. What relationship(s) would I like to enhance? What are some possible first steps?

38. As a kid, what did I dream of doing when I grew up?

39. What activities are so engaging, I lose track of time?

40. Who's the best leader I've ever had? What qualities made her/him so amazing?

41. When do I feel the most successful? Like I am in the right place, doing exactly what I'm supposed to be doing?

42. What are some small actions that, if I made them part of my daily routine, would make a positive difference?

43. What do I need to let go of (grudges, past frustrations, long-ago mistakes) in order to freely move forward in my work, leadership, and life?

44. If my favorite magazine asked to write a feature article about me a year from now, what would I want the story to be?

45. What distractions am I allowing into my days? How can I start to minimize them?

46. When I think of my whole life -- mind, body, spirit, career, relationships, etc. -- what do I need more of? Less of?

47. What are 5-10 accomplishments that I am really proud of?

48. What role does kindness play in my work, leadership, and life? How could I invite more in and express more?

49. How do I make a positive difference in others' lives? How could I do that even more?

50. What words do I want to come to mind when others think about me?

"

Journaling For

Attracting Love

"

If you're looking for a new love, or want to attract love in your current relationship, I want to share with you some powerful ways to use a journal to help you get there.

What is your Why?

What exactly do you want in a relationship? Why Now? Write it down. Why? Why do you want that? Write it down. Connecting with the 'why' behind your desires gives you the fuel of passion needed to birth your desires into reality.

Do you want to have a partner who will be "all in" and commit to being in a relationship? Why?

Do you want a partner who shares your passion for fitness? For a certain kind of music? Why?

Do you want someone who will go dancing with you? Why?

It's a journal exercise that helps you connect with your bottom line. It feeds the emotions and feelings that help bring your desires into existence.

Journaling Prompts To Attract Love

To attract love from someone else you must first love yourself. I know that's something you've likely heard before; it's true. How can you be putting out "attraction vibes" if you don't feel attractive? These prompts are designed to get you in touch with love in general. Pull out your journal and just get started.

Journal Prompts For Attracting Love

CHOOSE ONE PROMPT EACH DAY AND DEDICATE 5-10 MINUTES WRITING YOUR ANSWER. IF YOUR TIME RUNS LONGER BECAUSE YOU HAVE A LOT TO WRITE, SO BE IT. IF YOU CHOOSE MORE THAN ONE PROMPT SO BE IT....FREEDOM IS KEY.

1. My ideal partner is...

2. I feel loved when...

3. Brainstorm ways I can put myself "out there" and ready to be with my ideal partner...

4. I show love to my ideal partner by...

5. My ideal partner shows me love by...

6. I am lovable because...

7. My biggest struggle in loving myself is...

8. I am willing to release...

9. I am willing to receive...

10. I am...

11. Love is...

If you haven't tried journaling to attract love into your life, I urge you to try some of these techniques; they work. I would love to hear your experiences with them.

WHICH LIMITING BELIEFS DO YOU NEED TO OVERCOME?"

If you allow limiting beliefs to thrive inside your head, they'll prevent you from manifesting the things you want... so let's crush those little suckers!

A few common limiting beliefs are:
1. I don't deserve to be loved.
2. My goals are impossible to achieve.
3. I'll never have enough money.

Once you identify the limiting beliefs that are holding you back, try to re-frame them in your journal entry. Here are examples of the above beliefs re-framed:
1. I am deserving of love.
2. I will achieve my goals.
3. I will make lots of money.

Write the positive statements down, and write them every day until you start to believe them. If you notice a limiting belief coming back into your conscious thoughts, question it. Refute it with the opposite positive statement. And then, put it to rest. Don't give the limiting belief any more of your attention.

When you focus on the positive, you'll attract positivity. When you focus on your goals, you'll attract success... notice a pattern here?

Journaling For

Positive
Thinking

By now you are hopefully enjoying journaling and seeing your perspective of life evolve right in front of you.

Remember even if you only spend 5 to 10 minutes per day writing in your journal, you'll notice improvements in your mindset over time!

THE POWER OF POSITIVE THINKING CAN CHANGE YOUR LIFE

Let me begin by explaining the meaning of positive thinking:

1. Positive thinking is a mental and emotional attitude that focuses on optimistic and positive thoughts and expects positive results.
2. People with a positive mentality look at the bright side of life and anticipate happiness, health, and success.
3. These people are confident that they will overcome any obstacle and difficulty they might face.

To take advantage of the power of positive thinking, you need to practice it. It is not enough just be aware of its existence or believe that it can work.

With a positive attitude we experience pleasant and happy feelings.

This brings brightness to the eyes, more energy, and more happiness. Our whole being broadcasts good will, happiness, and success.

This behavior affects our physical, emotional, and mental health in a beneficial way. Our body language shows the way we feel, we walk tall and we speak more confidently.

Did you Know that Negative and positive thinking are contagious?

We affect, and are affected by the people we meet, in one way or another. This happens instinctively and on a subconscious level, through words, thoughts, and feelings, and through body language.

Is it any wonder that we prefer to be around positive people and avoid negative people?

People are more disposed to help us if we are positive and in a good mood. Most people avoid anyone broadcasting negativity.

Negative thoughts, words, and attitude, create negative and unhappy feelings, moods, and behavior.

So, my question is are you a negative or positive person?

Are those around mostly positive or negative?

"Promise yourself success at the beginning of each day, and you'll be surprised how often things will turn out that way." – Norman Vincent Peale

The Benefits of Positive Thoughts and Gratitude

A positive mental attitude produces positive thoughts, which affect many aspects of life in a favorable way, career, success, health, and state of mind.

1. This attitude has a good effect on your mental health and emotional health, because it makes you more confident and happier, and less worried and anxious.

2. This kind of mindset reduces stress and anxiety. Less stress and anxiety mean better immunity system and improved physical health.

3. This state of mind makes you more optimistic, friendly, and considerate, and this improves your relations with people.

4. With this attitude, you program your mind to be aware of opportunities that can improve your life.

5. With this mental outlook, you feel more motivated, and can more easily motivate people to improve themselves and their life.

6. With a positive frame of mind there is faster recuperation, both physically and emotionally.

7. It helps you avoid negative self-talk and shift to positive self-talk.

8. This kind of outlook is one of the main keys to success since you expect constructive results in all areas of life.

9. A mental attitude that focuses on the good and on positive thoughts awakens positive emotions, drives away negative emotions, and positively affects the environment.

Benefits of Gratitude

- Improved physical, emotional physical, emotional, and social well-being.

- Greater optimism and happiness,

- Improved feelings of connection in times of loss or crises.

- Increased self-esteem.

- Heightened energy levels.

- Strengthened heart, immune system, and decreased blood pressure.

- Improved emotional and academic intelligence

- Expanded capacity for forgiveness

- Decreased stress, anxiety, depression, and headaches

- Improved self-care and greater likelihood to exercise

- Heightened spirituality -- ability to see something bigger than ourselves

- It promotes positive thinking patterns.

- It promotes empathy and compassion.

- It combats negative feelings.

- It encourages healthy lifestyle choices.

- It increases resilience.

- It increases happiness overall!

This list is not exhaustive. As your mindset shifts, other positive lifestyle changes will follow. That's why you should make journaling a part of your wellness routine!

Journal Prompts For Positive Thinking

CHOOSE ONE PROMPT EACH DAY AND DEDICATE 5-10 MINUTES WRITING YOUR ANSWER. IF YOUR TIME RUNS LONGER BECAUSE YOU HAVE A LOT TO WRITE, SO BE IT. IF YOU CHOOSE MORE THAN ONE PROMPT SO BE IT....FREEDOM IS KEY.

Here are prompts for your Positive Thinking Journal.

Being Grateful makes for a Positive Attitude and Mentality. So below you will find journal prompts for gratitude to foster that much needed positivity in your day to day life.

1. List 10 things you're grateful for.

2. List 10 abilities or skills you've been blessed with.

3. Write about something that has brought you joy recently.

4. Write about the best gift you ever received.

104

5. List 10 things you love about yourself.

6. Think of one person you love. Write why you're grateful to have that person in your life.

7. Gather photos of your loved ones and tape each one into a separate page in your gratitude journal. Underneath each photo, list some things you love about that person.

8. Think about a friend or family member who's been extra nice to you lately. List five reasons you have to thank them. Then, call that person and read off your list!

9. Think of three compliments you've received. Write about why you're thankful you received them.

10. Think about your skills and strengths. Write about why you're grateful for them.

11. List 5 aspects of your personality that you like.

12. Write three thank-you notes to people you're grateful for. Mail the letters!

13. Think of a special gift you could give to someone. (It does not have to cost money, but it needs to be personalized in some way.) Write your ideas down, pick your favorite one, and set an intention to either buy or make the gift.

14. Write about a lesson you learned that you're grateful for.

15. Write about the best day of your life.

16. Think about a time you witnessed a miracle in your life. Write about how grateful you are for it.

17. Write about a time you felt proud of yourself.

18. Write about your happy place.

19. List 10 things that make you feel relaxed and at ease.

20. List 20 little things you can celebrate in life.

21. Write about an experience that changed your life for the better.

22. Write about something you're looking forward to.

23. Write about an organization or charity you're thankful for.

24. List 10 things you can do to help others in the near future.

25. Think about a role model of yours. Write about why you look up to that person.

26. Write about a teacher or mentor you're grateful for.

27. List 5 aspects of your body that you're grateful for.

28. Write about a happy memory of yours.

29. List 10 things that make you smile.

30. Think of your favorite quote and write about why it inspires you.

31. Think of your favorite song and write about why you love it so much.

32. Write about a holiday you're grateful for.

33. Think about your favorite way to express yourself. Write why you're grateful for it.

34. Write why you're grateful for the present moment.

35. Think about which of your senses (sight, hearing, touch, smell, or taste) is your favorite. Write why you're grateful for it.

36. List the things you love about your home.

37. List 10 accomplishments you're grateful for.

38. Write why you're grateful for your time in the world.

39. List three positive intentions you can set for tomorrow.

40. Think about something you love doing. Write why you're grateful for it.

41. List three opportunities you've had in life that you're grateful for.

42. Imagine yourself waking up every day in a positive mindset. Write about the changes you need to make in order to start thinking that way.

43. Write the things you love most about the morning.

44. Write the things you love most about the evening.

45. Write about your favorite dessert or treat.

46. Think about one of your primary goals in life. Write about how you're grateful for the opportunity to achieve it.

47. Write about a trip you took in the past and why you're grateful for it.

48. List three of your core values and explain why you're grateful to have them.

49. Write about why you're grateful for your heritage.

50. Think about your favorite possession. Write about why you're thankful to have it.

51. Write about something you created that you're grateful for.

52. Write about your favorite season and the things you love about it.

53. Write down some things you love about the city you live in.

54. Think about your age. Write about why you're grateful to be living at your particular age.

55. Make a list of 100 things to be thankful for. (You can put anything on your list!)

Journaling For

Relationships & Marriage

Journal Prompts For Relationships & Marriage

CHOOSE ONE PROMPT EACH DAY AND DEDICATE 5-10 MINUTES WRITING YOUR ANSWER. IF YOUR TIME RUNS LONGER BECAUSE YOU HAVE A LOT TO WRITE, SO BE IT. IF YOU CHOOSE MORE THAN ONE PROMPT SO BE IT....FREEDOM IS KEY.

Relationships are the fabric of our being. We all have those around us who we love deeply. And those who we struggle with. These are 30 journal prompts plus a FREE printable that will help you to explore your relationships, whether it's with a spouse, partner, or friend, and how to love deeper in these relationships. Get out your bullet journal or regular journal and let's start loving more on our loved ones!

Remember, there are no rules in journaling!

These journal prompts are designed to help you honor that

space of being a better person to your loved ones, to examine their relationships with you, and what those steps are that you need to take to improve your relationships.

Prompts for Relationships

1. What am I most grateful for in a relationship?

2. Who am I most grateful for in my life?

3. What are the 3 things I admire most in my spouse/partner/friend?

4. What qualities do I believe are most important in a spouse/partner/friend?

5. How does my spouse/partner/friend make me feel loved?

6. How do I show true love to my spouse/partner/friend?

7. What are the best traits that I bring to a relationship?

8. How does my spouse/partner/friend make me a better person?

9. What does good communication look like to me?

10. How can I bring more love into my relationships?

11. What activities do I enjoy doing most with my spouse/partner/friend?

12. How do I support my spouse/partner/friend's goals and dreams?

13. How am I being supported? Is it enough? Why or why not?

14. List 3 compliments I'm going to give to my spouse/partner/friend every day this week.

15. I would like to improve my relationship with _____. Why?

16. Do I hold onto a grudge? Why or why not?

17. Do I gossip? How do I feel about gossiping?

18. How can I show up more authentically for my spouse/partner/friend?

19. Are any of my relationships challenging right now? If yes, why?

20. Am I being treated the way I should be? Why or why not?

21. What does forgiveness mean to me?

22. Who do I need to forgive? Why?

23. Does my spouse/partner/friend listen to me? Why or why not?

24. Do I actively listen to my spouse/partner/friend? How can I be a better listener?

25. Who are 5 people I admire most and why?

26. Who in my life right now needs more of my support?

27. Who are 3 people I should reach out to who I haven't spoken with in a while?

28. Do I have any relationships that need mending? What is my game plan?

29. Who do I need to say "I love you" to more?

30. What can I do to be a better friend to my loved ones?

31. What are three things I admire most about my spouse/partner/significant other?

32. How can I bring more love into my relationships?

33. Who do I rely on most for support and advice?

34. Who drives me crazy, but I love anyway?

35. Describe the last piece of advice I received that was meaningful.

36. What are my S/P/SO's dreams?

37. When do we have the most fun together?

38. What do I do to actively support my S/P/SO's goals?

39. List three words that describe my S/P/SO.

40. When is the last time I did something nice for someone just for the sake of being nice?

41. Who do I need to set healthy boundaries with?

42. When was the last time I said, "I love you." to my S/P/SO?

43. What are the best parts of the current relationships I have in my life?

44. Who was kind to me today?

45. Describe a recent compliment given to me.

46. Who are my favorite people and why?

47. What relationship would I like to improve/develop over the next 6 months?

48. Who do I consider to be my closest friend and why?

49. How can I change and enhance how I communicate?

50. Who is the last person I said, "I love you" to?

51. Is there anyone in my life that I need to forgive? Explore the details of who, why, how, etc. of forgiveness.

52. List 5 people I'm most grateful to have in my life.

53. How do I feel when my S/P/SO walks into the room?

54. Do I have a relationship in my life that needs mending?

55. What is my Love Language? Explore the **"5 Love Languages"** by Gary Chapman.

56. How can I listen more to those in my life?

57. Who makes me laugh out loud when we're together?

58. Describe what love means do me.

59. List 5 people that have made a positive impact on my life.

60. Who is the most supportive of my goals? Have I told that person how much I appreciate them?

Journaling For

Managing Anger

L let's face it parenting is not a walk in the park, that is why it is important to journal about anger because most anger stems from childhood experiences.

Journaling is a really good way to help parents sort out their thoughts and make sense of how they are feeling from moment to moment.

Journaling can also help parents re-organize priorities when parenting life seems to get in the way and they are overwhelmed with just surviving and juggling everything.

Journal Prompts Managing Anger

CHOOSE ONE PROMPT EACH DAY AND DEDICATE 5-10 MINUTES WRITING YOUR ANSWER. IF YOUR TIME RUNS LONGER BECAUSE YOU HAVE A LOT TO WRITE, SO BE IT. IF YOU CHOOSE MORE THAN ONE PROMPT SO BE IT....FREEDOM IS KEY.

Take your journal and these prompts in the bathroom, in the car, outside on the patio and begin writing.

1. The best part of my day & why

2. One thing I would like to accomplish in the next 30 days

3. The most dreaded part of my day & why

4. 7 things I'm grateful for from the past week

5. I wish I was better at ____

6. One way I can use my talents to benefit my family

7. A financial goal for the next month

8. 3 ways to bloom where I am planted

9. The best recent show or movie I've seen & why I'm drawn to it

10. A relationship in my life I'd like to improve

11. I feel most relaxed when...

12. I feel most stressed when...

13. A movie or book character I can relate to

14. A quality I really value in myself

15. A quality I really value in my child

16. An aspect of my health that needs attention

17. A recent loving thing I did for myself & why it was needed

18. A recent disagreement with someone and what I learned

19. A recent compliment I received and how it made me feel

20. Something I'm really looking forward to in the next 30 days

21. A recent news event and how I felt about it

22. Something I could do to be more neighbourly

23. A way I can help my child grow in confidence

24. A way in which I wish my child was more independent

25. A mom-friendship I really value & why

26. Something I wish I had more time for

27. A recent dream that troubled me & how it made me feel

28. An aspect of parenting that I'm really good at

29. The love languages of my children

30. How I show my kids I love them

31. Who are what inspires you to be a better parent?

32. What are your current goals are a parent?

33. What are you current goals for your child(ren)?

34. What do you want your child(ren) to remember most about their childhood?

35. Fill in the blank. As a parent I _____.

36. List your top 3 strengths and how they impact your family.

37. List your 3 weaknesses and how they impact your family.

38. What did your child do today that was new in their development and growth? How did this impact you?

39. What triggered your mom rage today? Was it a messy home, lack of self-care, mommy comparisons and etc?

40. What is the best and worst parenting advice that you have ever received? Why?

41. Write a letter to your child for age 10, 15 or 20.

42. How do you recharge your mind and body? How can you improve upon this?

43. What is your favorite thing to do with your child(ren)?

44. Are your expectations of yourself too high? Why or why not?

45. Name one thing that you feel is keeping you from being the best parent that you can be to your child(ren). How can you change it?

46. What makes your child feel most loved?

47. Which of your child's behaviors triggers you the most? Why? How can you change your response the trigger?

48. Who do you trust for mom advice? Why?

49. Write a letter to yourself on the accomplishments and advancements you have had in your parenting journey.

50. Write a plan for a self-care day for your child(ren). Example, bubble bath with herbs, fruit bowl while in bubble bath with soft music playing.

51. What piece of advice would you give another mother? Are you able to share it in a positive way with the mother?

52. In what ways can your partner or co-parent provide support in your positive parenting journey? Are you able to share this in a positive way with your partner/co-parent?

Journaling For

Depression

One of the ways to deal with any overwhelming emotion is to find a healthy way to express yourself.

This makes journaling a helpful tool in managing your mental health especially

- Manage anxiety
- Reduce stress
- Cope with depression

Journaling for depression reveals your most private fears, thoughts, and feelings that might trigger depression. Below are prompts that can help you with managing emotions related to depression.

Journal Prompts For Depression

CHOOSE ONE PROMPT EACH DAY AND DEDICATE 5-10 MINUTES WRITING YOUR ANSWER. IF YOUR TIME RUNS LONGER BECAUSE YOU HAVE A LOT TO WRITE, SO BE IT. IF YOU CHOOSE MORE THAN ONE PROMPT SO BE IT....FREEDOM IS KEY.

Please NOTE:

These prompts are not treatment, they are educational questions to help you gather your thoughts on what you are feeling and thinking. Please discuss your answers with a mental health professional if you suffer from depression or to get support with your depression.

Remember the most important thing is that you journal regularly.

1. Write down 3 things you achieved today.

2. Write 3 things you are thankful for.

3. When were you last not depressed? What is different in your life then and now?

4. Write about the happiest time in your life.

5. What are 3 new hobbies you would like to try?

6. What is a part of yourself you are unhappy with – how can you work on improving this?

7. What is a goal you are working towards?

8. What are you doing to work towards that goal?

9. Name 1 event that troubles you and you want to work on letting go of.

10. What area of your life are you most unhappy with? (friends, career, relationship, financial)

11. How can you start making changes to improve this area?

12. When is the last time you did something nice for yourself?

13. What are your interests?

14. Talk about a time you helped someone.

15. Talk about a time you helped a stranger.

16. What is something that you are looking forward to?

17. What is something you can plan, so you will look forward to it?

18. What is 1 habit you would like to stop?

19. What is 1 habit you would like to start?

20. What is your favorite inspirational quote?

21. How can you make more time for those interests?

22. How would your perfect life look?

23. Who is someone who is negative, and you would like to spend less time with?

24. Who are people that have a positive effect on your life, and you would like to spend more time with?

25. Who inspires you?

26. What is your favorite uplifting song?

27. Name something you need to forgive your younger self for.

28. What motivates you?

29. What is 1 self-care idea you are going to do for yourself every day?

30. What is 1 way in which you can reward yourself when you accomplish something

31. Where do you want to be in 10 years' time.

32. How do you think your life would be different if you were not depressed?

33. What are your favorite techniques to de-stress yourself?

34. Name 3 techniques you can try next time you feel depressed.

35. What are your favorite things to do when you feel depressed?

36. Write about your values and morals.

37. Is there any way you could change your life to live more in line with those morals?

38. What are 5 things in your life you are thankful for?

39. How would your best friend describe you?

40. What is your perfect career?

41. Do you have any secret quirky talents?

42. How can you make changes in your life to achieve this?

43. What have you learned through having depression?

44. Who can you talk to about your depression?

45. Make a list of 3 Mental Health books you would like to read this year.

46. What are 3 Mental Health apps you want to try?

47. Make a list of 10 Ted Talks For mental health that you would like to watch.

48. How would you describe depression to someone who hasn't experienced it?

49. Which of these depression quotes resonated mostly with you?

50. Do you think that people should talk more about their Mental Health?

51. Do you think that depression can be overcome?

52. What would you say to a friend who is suffering with depression?

53. What are things that trigger your depression?

54. How can you minimize or avoid these triggers?

55. What is 1 change you can make in your life to avoid depression in the future?

Journaling For

Anxiety

C hallenging your thoughts can help you relieve anxiety. Journaling helps you see that things are less likely to happen than you think, or they are not as bad as you think they could be.

Below are prompts that can help you with managing emotions related to anxiety. Please NOTE: These prompts are not treatment, they are educational questions to help you gather your thoughts on what you are feeling and thinking.

Please discuss your answers with a mental health professional if you suffer from depression or to get support with your anxiety.

Journal Prompts For Anxiety

CHOOSE ONE PROMPT EACH DAY AND DEDICATE 5-10 MINUTES WRITING YOUR ANSWER. IF YOUR TIME RUNS LONGER BECAUSE YOU HAVE A LOT TO WRITE, SO BE IT. IF YOU CHOOSE MORE THAN ONE PROMPT SO BE IT....FREEDOM IS KEY.

Remember the most important thing is that you journal regularly.

1. Today, I am thankful for.....

2. My favorite accomplishment it....

3. I am anxious when....

4. I felt sad when....

5. What is one thing I wish I could change...

6. My happiest memory is...

7. What's been bugging me lately?

8. Make a list of 15 things you love about yourself...

9. My favorite body part is...

10. One way I could love myself more is....

11. My Childhood hero was _____ and I am similar to them in these ways _____.

12. What is your best quality?

13. Write a letter to one of your parents. (You do not have to give it to them.)

14. Make a list of 10 quotes that inspire you

15. Make a list of 20 things you are grateful for.

16. What is one way your depression or anxiety has held you back this week? What could you do to change that?

17. Write yourself a letter forgiving you for something that has happened in your past.

18. Create a Brainstorm list of activities to reduce your stress and anxiety. Make a plan to add at least 3 activities to your schedule this week.

19. Write a letter to your younger self. What advice can you give them to better navigate their mental health?

20. The last time I felt this way, I...

21. What is one thing you wish you had said no to? Why didn't you? What impact did it have on your experience?

22. Write a review about your favorite book or movie and why it resonates with you so deeply.

23. Make a schedule for your perfect day. Take one of these things and do it sometime this week.

24. What is something I need to let go of? Why am I holding onto it?

25. Describe your ideal bedroom. The way it looks, the smell, the feel of the sheets, comfort, and overall atmosphere there.

26. What does self-care mean to you? How do practice this in your daily life?

27. Write down three things that cause you anxiety. Brainstorm 1–2 ways you can combat these triggers when they come up.

28. What are 3 things about yourself you wish others knew? How could you share these things with others more?

29. Choose an Inspiration word for the week. What does it mean to you? And how can you live your life this week with that word in mind?

30. Make a list of 17 accomplishments you've made that you are proud of.

31. Write about five things that you are grateful for today. This will provide you with a visual representation of some of the good things in your life, and can help reduce the impact of negative thoughts.

32. Describe the moment in which you began to feel anxious. What were you doing? Where were you going? What did you eat that day? Analyzing this situation can help you identify triggers.

33. If someone, in particular, is causing you fear or anxiety, use your journal to write them a letter that you never intend to send. It can be therapeutic to get your thoughts out.

34. List the top five emotions that you are feeling today.

35. Write about what scares you the most, and explain why you are afraid of it. This can help you identify what is causing you anxiety, and you may be able to use your own reason and logic to sort through it.

36. Spend five or ten minutes doing a stream-of-consciousness journal entry. In the event that you are feeling anxious and you don't understand why you may uncover it through this freeform style of writing.

37. Describe your bedtime routine, then consider how that routine may be impacting your ability to fully rest at night. At the end of the journal entry, write down simple changes that you may be able to make to alleviate stress before bedtime.

38. Write about your favorite memory from childhood. If you are feeling sad or anxious, you may find that this nostalgic look back on happier times helps you reset.

39. Switch up your journaling process by using a pen in your favorite color. Then, write about why you chose that pen and why it is your favorite color.

40. Think about one moment in your day that always brings you joy. Describe it in detail, and explain why that is your favorite moment of the day. In times of stress, focus on that moment.

41. Write down three long-term goals that you have, and then make a list of short-term goals that you can realistically achieve that will help you work toward your long-term goals. This can help you feel less stressed about what lies ahead.

42. Fill in the blank: I was anxious today because:

43. Write a fictional story about a character who is struggling with anxiety, and make sure that the character finds a resolution. Consider this solution, and see if it can apply to your own life.

44. Consider the past several months or years, and write about the time when you were experiencing the most anxiety. Describe what steps you took to overcome that anxiety. By recognizing that you can overcome it, you may be able to cope better in the future.

45. Write a love poem about yourself.

Journaling For

Stress & Anxiety

A s we have talked about so far journaling is an amazing tool for mental health, wellbeing, business and productivity. The journal has been in use for thousands of years. Much of the earth's history comes from early journal entries.

I know that with business if we don't address our anxieties, anxiety tends to get in the way. I have had to be very intentional and pay attention to managing my anxiety.

Try not to stress over your journal-

These anxiety journal writing prompts will help get you started, but don't feel pressure to write 15 pages or complete every single prompt. You don't even have to stay on topic! Anxiety and Depression are not linear, and your journaled thoughts don't need to be either.

Start with writing for just 5–10 minutes in a sitting. Setting a timer can help a lot. Or if you feel like 5–10 minutes isn't a good measure try to write 2 pages.

Journal Prompts For Stress & Anxiety

CHOOSE ONE PROMPT EACH DAY AND DEDICATE 5-10 MINUTES WRITING YOUR ANSWER. IF YOUR TIME RUNS LONGER BECAUSE YOU HAVE A LOT TO WRITE, SO BE IT. IF YOU CHOOSE MORE THAN ONE PROMPT SO BE IT....FREEDOM IS KEY.

Prompts for Anxiety and Depression To Get You Started-

1. Today, I am thankful for.....

2. My favorite accomplishment it....

3. I am anxious when....

4. I felt sad when....

5. What is one thing I wish I could change...

6. My happiest memory is...

7. What's been bugging me lately?

8. Make a list of 15 things you love about yourself...

9. My favorite body part is...

10. One way I could love myself more is....

11. My Childhood hero was _____ and I am similar to them in these ways _____.

12. What is your best quality?

13. Write a letter to one of your parents. (You do not have to give it to them.)

14. Make a list of 10 quotes that inspire you

15. Make a list of 20 things you are grateful for.

16. What is one way your depression or anxiety has held you back this week? What could you do to change that?

17. Write yourself a letter forgiving you for something that has happened in your past.

18. Create a Brainstorm list of activities to reduce your stress and anxiety. Make a plan to add at least 3 activities to your schedule this week.

19. Write a letter to your younger self. What advice can you give them to better navigate their mental health?

20. The last time I felt this way, I...

21. What is one thing you wish you had said no to? Why didn't you? What impact did it have on your experience?

22. Write a review about your favorite book or movie and why it resonates with you so deeply.

23. Make a schedule for your perfect day. Take one of these things and do it sometime this week.

24. What is something I need to let go of? Why am I holding onto it?

25. Describe your ideal bedroom. The way it looks, the smell, the feel of the sheets, comfort, and overall atmosphere there.

26. What does self-care mean to you? How do practice this in your daily life?

27. Write down three things that cause you anxiety. Brainstorm 1–2 ways you can combat these triggers when they come up.

28. What are 3 things about yourself you wish others knew? How could you share these things with others more?

29. Choose an Inspiration word for the week. What does it mean to you? And how can you live your life this week with that word in mind?

30. Make a list of 17 accomplishments you've made that you are proud of.

31. What was the most difficult experience you had before, and how were you able to overcome it? Recalling challenging times makes us see how far we've come and might just inspire us to be grateful for all that has happened.

32. **List three things that scare you the most, and the reasons why.** Facing the things that scare us lessens their power to make us anxious.

33. **Recall three positive things that happened to you today and write them down. Be as detailed as possible.** Recalling positive things that happened in the day improves mood and motivation.

34. **Reply to your inner critic's opinions about your actions and decisions.** If it's calling your attention to all the wrong things you've done, this is the time to focus on the right things you've accomplished, and to dismiss your inner critic's poor opinion of you.

35. **How are you feeling right now? Describe how you feel in writing.** Do you like how you're feeling right now? If not, how would you like to feel? What can you do to change how you're feeling?

36. **List down all of the things that you're worried about right now. Make the list as long as possible.** Putting all your worries out into the open prevents them from occupying too much space in your head.

37. **Write a letter to three of your greatest supporters.** Think of the people who support you. Choose three of them. Then write a letter to each one detailing the ways they support you and telling them how much you appreciate them. You don't have to mail the letters if you don't want to.

38. **What are the three things you'd love to be doing for the rest of your life?** Writing down the things you'd love to do even without receiving any compensation for them will help you reconnect with your passions.

39. **Make a list of the compliments you've received from others.** Writing down the compliments you've gotten from others helps boost confidence and gives hope.

40. **What are five moments in your life when you can say you were truly happy?**

41. **Think back to a moment when you experienced failure. What lessons can you take from it?** Failure is necessary. It is considered the greatest teacher we'll have in this life. Without it, we will be incapable of reaching for greater achievements.

42. **Write a letter to yourself. Make it a love letter.** Discover how uniquely wonderful you are as you write about the admirable qualities you have.

43. **If you're prone to anxiety attacks, write down all the strategies you've used in the past that helped you cope with a flare up.** This list will help you realize that you've always managed to survive an attack, and will give you hope to overcome the condition.

44. **Is your anxiety trying to tell you something? What is it?** Taking a closer look at your anxiety

helps you discover the underlying reasons for your anxious thoughts, and hopefully motivates you to deal with them in a healthy way.

45. **Describe the thing or situation that you look forward to every day.** Writing about things that give us joy anchors us and gives us strength to move forward.

46. **List three of the greatest lessons you've been given by your anxiety.** Having anxiety changes our outlook about life. Writing about this can help you discover the new you that's emerging.

47. **List at least 10 activities you can do to take better care of yourself.** This is an action plan to help you remember that you (your health and well-being) are important.

48. **What values are important to you?** Knowing which values you think are important helps you define your personal boundaries.

49. **List down your anxiety triggers.** Knowing your triggers can help lessen the effect of symptoms during a flare up, or completely prevent them.

50. **Think of someone who has caused you pain. Write him or her a letter of forgiveness.** Letting go of anger and resentment frees up our energy to be happier and more present in our own lives.

Journaling For

Financial Prosperity

Journal Prompts For Financial Prosperity

CHOOSE ONE PROMPT EACH DAY AND DEDICATE 5-10 MINUTES WRITING YOUR ANSWER. IF YOUR TIME RUNS LONGER BECAUSE YOU HAVE A LOT TO WRITE, SO BE IT. IF YOU CHOOSE MORE THAN ONE PROMPT SO BE IT....FREEDOM IS KEY.

1. Describe your relationship with money in five words or less.

2. What was your money story growing up?

3. What does it mean to you to have "not enough" money?

4. What does it mean to you to have "too much" money?

5. What, to you, is the purpose of money?

6. How do you feel about money today?

7. How would you like to feel about money?

147

8. What is your biggest fear in relation to money?

9. How does money bring you joy?

10. When have you felt at your richest?

11. What is the largest sum of money you've ever received?

12. What, in your opinion, is a "good" amount of money to earn?

13. What is the most money you've ever spent on something?

14. Imagine you inherited $5000 from a distant relative with the condition you had to spend it on something other than yourself. What would you do with the money?

15. What would you do if you ran out of money tomorrow?

16. What is the best or most helpful piece of advice you've heard about money?

17. What is the worst or least helpful piece of advice?

18. How do you talk about money with friends and family? (Do you?)

19. What would you like your financial life to look like in 10 years' time?

20. What is one thing you could do today to improve your financial life?

21. What are four money manifestations (or financial achievements) that you're grateful for right now?

22. Where do you see your relationship with money in 6 months? One year? Five years? Ten years?

23. What do you most enjoy about your current financial situation?

24. Is there anything in life that you need help regarding your money? What do you need? Who could you ask?

25. When's the last time you encountered a new opportunity to manifest more money?

26. What do you need more of in your life?

27. What do you need less of in your life?

28. Pick five words to describe your attitude toward money.

29. What is the best piece of advice you've ever received when it comes to money?

30. What's the best piece of money advice you've ever received – that you didn't take?

31. Describe one of your most memorable experiences surrounding money.

31. What is your most profitable talent, trait or skill?

32. Who are you most thankful for in your life and why?

33. What financial advice would you, today, give to yourself five years ago?

34. If your future self could give you three pieces of money advice, what would it be?

35. Do you compare your financial situation to anyone else's? Are you jealous? Why?

36. Is there something that could make you more money, yet you're avoiding getting started because of fear?

37. What can you do today to make it better than yesterday?

38. If you've made money mistakes that you still regret to this day, what did you learn from them?

39. What do you value most in life?

40. What are your biggest goals right now?

41. How are you moving toward achieving your biggest goals?

42. What accomplishments are you most proud of?

43. What thing would you do if you knew you couldn't fail?

44. Describe your perfect day in great detail.

45. What are three of your favorite affirmations or mantras? If you don't have any, create some.

46. How do you practice financial self-care? How do you care for and respect your money?

47. What do you want your legacy to be?

48. What issue from your past is holding you back from attracting more money?

49. Which types of things do you find annoying with respect to money?

50. What activities brought you joy and made you feel alive as a child?

51. What activities bring you joy and make you feel alive? Do they require large amounts of money?

52. Where would you go on your dream vacation if money wasn't an object?

53. Who do you look up to as a role model, and why?

54. What's your ideal way to generate income? Your dream job?

55. What word would you use to describe yourself, and why?

56. How did your darkest moments in life influence your current financial situation?

57. Set a three-minute timer and write whatever comes to mind.

58. Describe one toxic person, thing, or habit that you need to let go of to boost your income.

59. In what areas of your life *not* related to money, would you like to see change or growth that might *lead to* more money flowing your way?

60. Are you happy with where you live? If not, what would you prefer?

61. What do you believe in?

62. If you knew you were going to die in exactly 30 days, how would you live your life?

63. What brings you the most peace?

64. How do you contribute to the good of the world? If you had unlimited money, would this change?

65. What stresses you out the most?

66. Are you being true to yourself and living authentically? Why or why not?

67. How do you enjoy spending your free time? Would this change if you had unlimited money?

68. How do you express your love for others? Would this change with more money?

69. When in life did you have the strongest relationship with your money?

70. What is your first memories about money?

71. When it comes to money, I believe...

72. What activities am I doing that are responsible for 80% of my financial results?

73. What activities and people are causing 80% of my negative results/emotions/beliefs about money/wealth? How could I change those negatives into positives?

74. Write a letter to money, as if they were a person, telling him/her what kind of relationship you would like to have with them.

75. If you received 10 million dollars in cash, but had to spend it within the next 24 hours, how would you spend it? Be very, very specific – down to the dollar and cents!

76. When I retire, I will...

"

Journaling For

The
Grateful
Heart

"

Journal Prompts For The Greatful Heat

CHOOSE ONE PROMPT EACH DAY AND DEDICATE 5-10 MINUTES WRITING YOUR ANSWER. IF YOUR TIME RUNS LONGER BECAUSE YOU HAVE A LOT TO WRITE, SO BE IT. IF YOU CHOOSE MORE THAN ONE PROMPT SO BE IT....FREEDOM IS KEY.

1. Blessings in my life that I'm grateful for.

2. Am I thankful more often than not? If not, why?

3. What areas of my life affect my gratitude?

4. How can I demonstrate my gratitude to God?

5. Search the word "gratitude" in a concordance & meditate on it.

6. Is there anything in my life I'm taking for granted?

7. People in my life that I'm blessed with.

8. Write a prayer thanking God for these special persons in your life.

9. I'm grateful for my salvation because...

10. My initial response to problems is to give thanks or have self-pity?

11. Can I go a month without shopping for wants?

12. Do I tend to focus more on what I have or what I don't have?

13. Meditate on Psalm 9:1.

14. God is good because...

15. A grateful heart is a happy heart. What are your thoughts on this?

16. The biggest blessing in my life is?

17. Things in my life I'm grateful for that didn't happen as planned.

18. Ways in which the LORD protected me.

19. Write down a verse about thanksgiving.

20. Read and meditate on Philippians 4.

21. Am I content in the good and bad times?

22. The "little" things that make me happy.

23. Today I'm grateful for...

24. Advice given to me that I'm thankful for.

25. Ways in which I show my gratitude towards others.

26. Something in nature that you're thankful for.

27. I'm thankful for prayer because...

28. I'm thankful for the Bible because...

29. Even if I don't have what I want, I'm grateful because...

30. Write a prayer of worship to God.

Journaling For

New
Beginnings

Journal Prompts For New Beginnings

CHOOSE ONE PROMPT EACH DAY AND DEDICATE 5-10 MINUTES WRITING YOUR ANSWER. IF YOUR TIME RUNS LONGER BECAUSE YOU HAVE A LOT TO WRITE, SO BE IT. IF YOU CHOOSE MORE THAN ONE PROMPT SO BE IT....FREEDOM IS KEY.

1. My verse theme for this year and how I want to apply to my life.

2. What new God-glorifying habits do I want to adopt this year?

3. What non-God- glorifying habits do I want to get rid of?

4. Ways in which I want to grow closer to God.

5. What I want my daily devotional time to look like.

6. Struggles I want to overcome.

7. People I want to pray for & why.

8. World issues I want to pray about & why.

9. Idols in my life that I want to get rid of.

10. Ways in which I want to grow Spiritually.

11. Sins that I need to confess to God.

12. Bible book (s) I plan to study more in-depth & why.

13. Spiritual, mental & physical toxins to remove from my life.

14. What is my Spiritual life lacking?

15. I'm grateful to God for...

16. Song lyrics that speak deeply to me.

17. A powerful Christian quote that speaks to me.

18. Christian book(s) I want to read & short description.

19. Ways in which I plan to witness to others.

20. How can I have more self-control this year?

21. What Spiritual battles am I fighting?

22. Distractions I need to get rid of to spend more time with God:

23. Journal about the fruits of the Spirit (Galatians 5:22)

24. How can I be more patient this year?

25. How can I be more thankful this year?

26. How can I be more joyful this year?

27. How can I find more peace this year?

28. How can I be more loving this year?

29. How can I be more kind and gentle this year?

30. How can I be more faithful this year?

31. A prayer of praise to God.

"

Journaling For

Building Resillience

"

Journal Prompts For Building Resillience

CHOOSE ONE PROMPT EACH DAY AND DEDICATE 5-10 MINUTES WRITING YOUR ANSWER. IF YOUR TIME RUNS LONGER BECAUSE YOU HAVE A LOT TO WRITE, SO BE IT. IF YOU CHOOSE MORE THAN ONE PROMPT SO BE IT....FREEDOM IS KEY.

1. What is going well in your life right now?

2. What could be improved?

3. Do you have a current morning routine? If you did, what would you want it to look like?

4. What are three things you are grateful for today?

5. What is something you did well in the last week?

6. What is something you are going to work on in the upcoming week?

7. What are your current short-term goals?

163

8. What are your current long-term goals?

9. What area of your life is getting the most time and attention right now? (Work, family, social life, money, fun, school, health, fitness, etc.)

10. What area of your life needs.a little more love and attention?

11. What fears do you have in life?

12. What scares you about the future?

13. What are you excited for in the future?

14. What are you still holding onto from the past?

15. Write a letter to your future self.

16. What would you do if you were not afraid?

17. What would you do with your life if money were no object? ...

Journaling For

Healing From Hurt

Journal Prompts For Healing From Hurt

CHOOSE ONE PROMPT EACH DAY AND DEDICATE 5-10 MINUTES WRITING YOUR ANSWER. IF YOUR TIME RUNS LONGER BECAUSE YOU HAVE A LOT TO WRITE, SO BE IT. IF YOU CHOOSE MORE THAN ONE PROMPT SO BE IT....FREEDOM IS KEY.

1. Is there someone in my life that I need to forgive?

2. How do I deal with hurt and pain?

3. How have I made pain, bitterness, and anger an idol in my life?

4. What is preventing me from pouring my heart out to God?

5. What does Scripture say about forgiving others?

6. Write a letter to someone who is hurting.

7. God heals by...

8. I want to live in freedom because...

9. I feel God's embrace the most when...

10. Lord, steady my anxious heart when...

11. What God told me lately...

12. The people in your life who have comforted and supported you.

13. God is GOOD because...

14. Scripture that comforts me.

15. God has manifested Himself in me through...

16. The differences I see when I pray vs. when I don't.

17. Something beautiful I saw today...

18. I find encouragement in...

19. Bible character I admire for their strength.

20. A strong and faithful person I know.

21. I can show Christ's love to someone today by...

22. I saw God today in...

23. Ways the Lord has provided for me.

24. Ways I can stop having self-pity.

25. I feel empowered when...

26. How can I use pain and hurt for God's glory?

27. Write an encouraging letter to yourself.

28. Write a prayer of worship to God.

Journaling For

Pursuing A Joyful Life

Journal Prompts For Pursuing a Joyful Life

CHOOSE ONE PROMPT EACH DAY AND DEDICATE 5-10 MINUTES WRITING YOUR ANSWER. IF YOUR TIME RUNS LONGER BECAUSE YOU HAVE A LOT TO WRITE, SO BE IT. IF YOU CHOOSE MORE THAN ONE PROMPT SO BE IT....FREEDOM IS KEY.

1. What is joy?

2. What brings me joy?

3. How can I have a more joyful life?

4. People in my life that bring me joy and why.

5. Search the word "joy" in a concordance & meditate on it.

6. What is the difference between happiness and joy?

7. Write down the many ways in which the LORD brings you joy.

8. Do I have any misconceptions about joy?

9. Read, meditate, and journal 1 Peter 1:8-9.

10. Write the lyrics of a song that bring you joy.

11. Something you experienced today that brought you joy

12. The world's definition of joy vs. what the Bible says.

13. Explain how you feel when you're joyous.

14. The joy of the LORD is...

15. Sharing the Gospel with others brings me joy because...

16. Journal Psalm 30:5

17. How would you bring joy to someone who has the blues?

18. Write a short poem on the LORD's joy.

19. How is gratitude and joy related?

20. I'm the most joyful when...

21. When I am down, I know the LORD can bring me joy because...

22. The joy of the LORD is my strength so...

23. Journal the fruits of the Spirit

24. Meditate on Romans 14:17

25. How I imagine joy in Heaven will be like.

26. Write a word of encouragement to yourself.

27. Prayer brings me peace and joy because...

28. Past experiences where I lacked joy.

29. What I have learned about rejoicing.

30. Ways in which fellowship brings joy.

31. Write a prayer of worship to God.

Journaling For

Breaking
Pride

Journal Prompts For Breaking Pride

CHOOSE ONE PROMPT EACH DAY AND DEDICATE 5-10 MINUTES WRITING YOUR ANSWER. IF YOUR TIME RUNS LONGER BECAUSE YOU HAVE A LOT TO WRITE, SO BE IT. IF YOU CHOOSE MORE THAN ONE PROMPT SO BE IT....FREEDOM IS KEY.

1. How much do I struggle with pride?

2. Things that offend me very much...

3. What are the reasons why these things offend me?

4. Do I tend to get offended easily?

5. Do I find it difficult to accept when I'm wrong?

6. What does the Bible say about pride? (Write out verses & meditate on them).

7. Do I struggle to apologize? If so, what can I do to change this?

8. How does pride affect my life and my relationship with God?

9. Things I regret doing and saying out of pride.

10. Write a prayer about letting go of pride.

11. Read, meditate, and journal James 4:6.

12. List ways in which you can practice humility daily.

13. How does pride lead me to other sins?

14. How badly do I want to get rid of the pride in my life?

15. How am I hurting others with my pride?

16. Am I holding back from forgiving someone out of pride?

17. How are pride and self-righteousness related?

18. Am I self-righteous? What can I do about it?

19. How does pride prevent me from thinking clearly sometimes:

20. When I get offended how does pride make me react?

21. Write a prayer of surrender to God.

22. Does pride make me feel entitled?

23. What does God say about pride?

24. Do I feel distant from God because of pride?

25. How does constant prayer make me more humble?

26. Bible character who displayed humility and what can I learn from him/her?

27. Someone in my life who is humble.

28. Father, make me humble because...

29. Write letter to younger self about pride.

30. Share an act of humility you did recently.

Write a prayer of worship to God

Journaling For

Being Still

Journal Prompts For Being Still

CHOOSE ONE PROMPT EACH DAY AND DEDICATE 5-10 MINUTES WRITING YOUR ANSWER. IF YOUR TIME RUNS LONGER BECAUSE YOU HAVE A LOT TO WRITE, SO BE IT. IF YOU CHOOSE MORE THAN ONE PROMPT SO BE IT....FREEDOM IS KEY.

1. How can I hear God's voice?

2. What do I need to mute in my life in order to hear God's voice?

3. What does God's voice sound like?

4. An experience where I heard God's voice.

5. A prayer of thanksgiving.

6. A petition to God.

7. A song of praise.

8. A poem of God's love.

9. Journal a Bible verse about peace.

10. Journal a Bible verse about God's love.

11. How can I have peace in the midst of chaos?

12. What brings me peace?

13. How is my prayer life right now?

14. How can I spend more time with God?

15. How was Jesus' prayer life like?

16. What can I emulate from Jesus' prayer life?

17. Write out and meditate on Colossians 3:15.

18. How does gratitude bring me peace?

19. Replace entertainment for prayer time for one day & write about it.

20. Someone in my life who inspires me to pray more.

21. Describe ways in which the LORD speaks to me.

22. Ways in which the LORD makes His presence felt in my life.

23. What does God's presence feel like?

24. God is good because...

25. I cannot get enough of His presence because...

26. I see God in...

27. The attributes of God are...

28. When I meditate on God's goodness I...

29. Ways in which I can influence others to pray more and play less.

30. Write a prayer of worship to God.

Journaling For

Goal Setting

Journal Prompts For Goal Setting

CHOOSE ONE PROMPT EACH DAY AND DEDICATE 5-10 MINUTES WRITING YOUR ANSWER. IF YOUR TIME RUNS LONGER BECAUSE YOU HAVE A LOT TO WRITE, SO BE IT. IF YOU CHOOSE MORE THAN ONE PROMPT SO BE IT....FREEDOM IS KEY.

1. 5 goals I'd like to accomplish by the end of this month are.

2. The holiday season makes me feel because.

3. Something I need to be free from and surrender to God today is.

4. Produce your personal thoughts or beliefs regarding an event that happened in the news or media this week.

5. On a Scale of 1-10 my mental health is at a.... today because...

6. Write about a person or area of your life where you need to create better boundaries for your own health.

7. Write about a defining event that changed the course of your life and how it has impacted the person you've become.

8. Today my favorite Bible verse is... because...

9. 10 things that bring me joy are.

10. List 3 emotions you are currently feeling and what reasons you think have contributed to these emotions.

11. What is one thing you want to be remembered for at the end of your life?

12. Write about an area of your life you need more support in right now.

13. Write about the biggest lesson you've learned from the life of someone who has passed away.

14. When I look in the mirror I see a woman/man who is.

15. Write about a favorite childhood memory.

16. If I had the ability to change one thing in the world. I'd hope to change.

17. Write about a bad decision you made in the past and what you've learned.

18. From 1-10, explain how much you're trusting God with your life right now.

19. In what ways are you different from the person you were 2 years ago?

20. Write about a goal or area of your life you need to be more committed to.

21. Write about a part of yourself most people don't see.

22. Pick a commitment you are dedicated to & reflect on why you're doing it.

23. Something I'd like to learn how to do next year is.

24. List 3 positive aspects of your relationship or life of being single right now.

25. List 20 words that come to your mind when you think of Jesus, Ready. go!

26. Note 4 emotions that come to your heart on Christmas day and why.

27. Write about the best piece of advice you've read/received this year.

28. Write a letter to your past self in the midst of a trial you faced last year.

29. Write what you've learned about being your age.

30. Review how you've done with the 5 goals you set on Day 1.

31. List 7 new habits you'd like to adapt in the new year.

Journaling For

Getting In
Touch With
Your Spiritual
Side

Journal Prompts For Getting In Touch With Your Spiritual Side

CHOOSE ONE PROMPT EACH DAY AND DEDICATE 5-10 MINUTES WRITING YOUR ANSWER. IF YOUR TIME RUNS LONGER BECAUSE YOU HAVE A LOT TO WRITE, SO BE IT. IF YOU CHOOSE MORE THAN ONE PROMPT SO BE IT....FREEDOM IS KEY.

1. What big things are you most grateful for right now?

2. What does spirituality mean to you?

3. Where does your spiritual streak show up in your daily life?

4. What do you believe makes the world a better place?

5. Do you believe you find your purpose or believe your purpose finds you?

6. Do you believe you have a soul? Why or why not?

7. What gives your life meaning today? What leaves you feeling purposeful?

8. What people, figures, or ideas have had the biggest impact on your spiritual life?

9. What is the number one problem you would like to solve in the world?

10. What do you think happens when we die?

11. How do you define wisdom? Where do you look for wisdom in your own life?

12. When have you felt most connected to your spiritual side?

13. What are some of the mantras or guiding principles you use in your spiritual life?

14. Do you believe more in serendipity or coincidence? Why?

15. What are some of your biggest unanswered questions in life?

"

Self-Interview
Questions

Knowing
Yourself
Better

"

1. How will your ideal you be like?

2. What is your biggest dream or goal?

3. What it means to you to achieve your dreams or goals, why are they worth fighting for?

4. What's in your way towards your dream?

5. Rank the most important things in your life (career, money, family, love, knowledge...)

6. What is the proportion of time dedicated to these items accordingly? (if most of your time is given to the less important things, you should think about reprioritizing your schedule)

7. If you have children, what would you recommend them to do or not do?

8. What are the 3 words that best describe yourself?

9. Has your personality changed since childhood? If so, why?

10. Is your personality similar to that of your parents?

11. What quality do you admire the most about yourself?

12. What is your biggest weakness?

Congratulations on purchasing this ultimate guide to journaling, an easy guide to help you pick a question and write. I have no doubt this will change your life. Make this a lifelong project of writing about your life.

Don't forget to check out the FOUR Lesson Course on Journaling to help you with the step by step guide to journaling titled:

The Ultimate Freedom Journaling Course on my website www.drstemmie.com that goes hand in hand with this guide.

DrStem Books and eBooks

eBOOKs now available on www.drstemmie.com under **"Empowerment Books"** tab.

These Books are available on **AMAZON** and Book Stores near you.

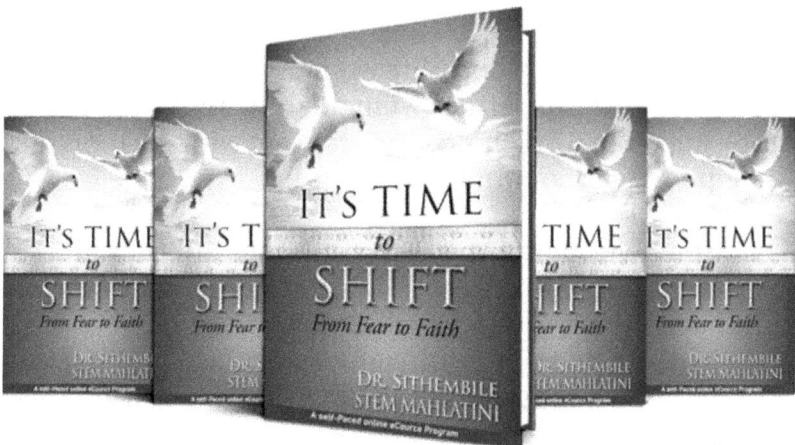

ABOUT THE EMPOWERMENT ACADEMY

The Empowerment Academy is a platform where women can have full access to life, career and business coaching, digital programs, eBooks, and tools for success in life, career and business with membership or individual bookings.

Corporations and Organizations can enjoy providing their employees with state-of-the-art wellness trainings, workshops, and digital programs. Trainings cover mental and health wellness, leaderships -Management skills, mindfulness, time management, organizational skills and more.

The Self-Care Workshops lift women up. The workshops are geared towards letting women know that they can be more, and each workshop provides them with the tools and the support to become more.

The Empowerment Academy provides all round real empowerment: with deep insight programs that address childhood issues, fears, mindfulness, stress management and success programs, with emphasis on an internal and positive change in each woman, so that she can find her passion, and purpose and change her life on her own terms.

THERE ARE TWO WOLVES INSIDE EACH OF US

ONE IS EVIL

ANGER
ENVY
SORROW
REGRET
GREED
ARROGANCE
SELF-PITY
GUILT
RESENTMENT
INFERIORITY
DECEPTION
FALSE PRIDE
SUPERIORITY
AND EGO

ONE IS GOOD

JOY
PEACE
HOPE
SERENITY
LOVE
HUMILITY
KINDNESS
PATIENCE
BENEVOLANCE
EMPATHY
GENEROSITY
TRUTH
COMPASSION
AND FAITH

Whichever WOLF wins is the one
YOU feed most.

Dr Stem (Sithembile Mahlatini, EdD, LCSW) Zimbabwe, Africa is an Employee Assistant Professional, Transitions Trainer, Speaker, Television & Radio Personality, Author and Licensed psychotherapist.

She is a Certified John Maxwell Leadership Trainer/Speaker, Certified Life- Career Coach, Passion test Facilitator and Josh Shipp Certified Youth Speaker.

As an author of 35 books she is Focused on three things: To Inspire, Influence and Impact.

Her joy is in helping you live a stress free lives and easily manifest wealth and health.

Email drstem14@gmail.com

People call Dr.Stem when they need to improve personal, professional, or business performance. Typically this is where she helps:

Help for individuals to;

- Get clear on their business and life goals
- Elevate their presents in their niche
- Connect More and Communicate Better in their relationships
- Manage Stress
- Manage the stress related to Career, Business, and relationship Decisions

Dr.Stem provides individual business coaching as well conduct workshops and training on the following:

- Stress Management and Leadership Trainings.
- Mindfulness Training.
- Relationship management.
- Managing change
- Balancing Work, Business and Life

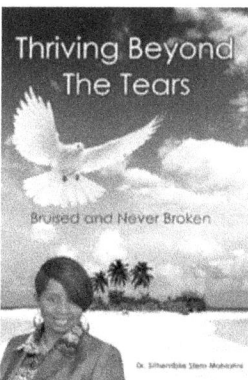

Read my Memoir easy download on my website or book on amazon or any bookstore near you.

E- Book Now available on www.drstemmie.com under Empowerment Books

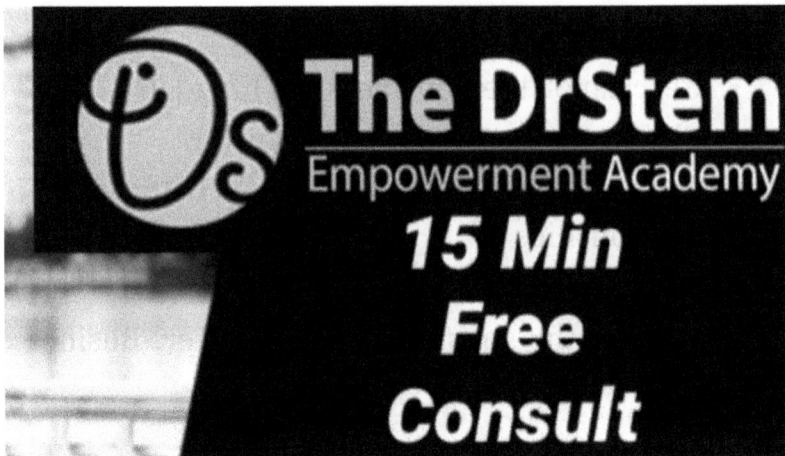

More Self Care Resources

Visit Our website at: www.drstemmie.com

Self-Care Workshops Relaxation

Join Our Memberships to Attend Workshops For Free or Pay as You Go for each Workshop.

For more information, including workshop topics and dates: Visit www.drstemmie.com

For one-on-one stress management coaching and counseling, please call 781 (254-1602) or email drstem14@gmail.com for more information.

Digital Courses and E Books

Visit our website www.drstemmie.com and go to Digital Courses Tab:
https://www.drstemmie.com/empowermentebooks

or the Parent TeenTab:
https://www.drstemmie.com/parentsteensebooks

Dr. Stem
Helping Other People Excel

DR. STEM SITHEMBILE MAHLATINI

www.drstemmie.com

200